THE SCATTERING

THE SCATTERING

IMAGES OF EMIGRANTS FROM AN IRISH COUNTY

EDITED BY ANNE JONES

TEXT BY RAY CONWAY

First published 2000
by
A. & A. Farmar
Beech House
78 Ranelagh Village
Dublin 6
Ireland
Tel: +353-1-496-3625
Fax: +353-1-497-0107
E-mail: afarmar@iol.ie
Web: farmarbooks.com

Design and typesetting Liam Furlong at Space (www.space.ie)
Illustrations scanned by The Scanning Shop
Printed and bound by Cahills

ISBN 1-899047-74-3 Paperback
ISBN 1-899047-77-8 Special Edition

To the memory of
Nora Sullivan and Pedro Scanlon

CONTENTS

A Message from the Patron

During the fourteen years I served as President of Ireland, I was invited to visit countries all over the world. As a native of Miltown Malbay in West Clare I was constantly amazed at how many fellow Clare people I met wherever I travelled. That's why a project such as this, to honour Clare people abroad, is so important. I hope that it will touch your heart as much as it has touched mine.

The emigrant experience has changed over the years. Once, letters home told of good times and great fortunes, even if this was not always the case. Visits home were infrequent, sometimes impossible. Now fast cars and ferries, e-mails and aeroplanes have made a world of difference.

This is an imaginative and timely project. The many stories that have emerged link us to a part of our heritage that, for too long, has gone unacknowledged. I see this book as an opportunity to recognise the enormous contribution our emigrants have made both by the sacrifice of their leaving and the generosity of their remittances.

Over the years the contribution of Clare's emigrants to the social and economic life of the county has been enormous. Their hard-earned money helped build new homes, schools and churches, fund small farms and businesses and educate siblings and cousins.

Tógann imircigh a gcultúr leo, ina dteanga agus ina gcuid ceoil. Ón Gorta ar aghaidh, is as na ceantair bhochta i gContae an Chláir a tháinig an imeacht mhór, sna háiteanna ina raibh an Ghaeilge mar theanga labhartha leis na mílte bliain. Ceann de na droch-thorthaí a bhí leis an imirce seo i gContae an Chláir, ná an Tost Mhór a d'fhág sé ina dhiaidh. Cé go bhfuil ár gceol ag teacht ar ais chuige féin le tríocha bliain anuas, is anois díreach atá ár nglór á aimsiú againn arís, agus go bhfuil an tabhacht a bhain lenár gcailliúnt á aithint againn.

What is truly striking about the project is that so much of the work has been done on a voluntary basis with proceeds from the publication going to aid a local charity, the St Vincent de Paul Society.

Dr. Patrick Hillery
President of Ireland
1976 – 1990

Acknowledgements

Shoot the Scattering Trust Limited gratefully acknowledges the assistance of the following sponsors:

Aer Lingus

Aer Rianta

AIB Better Ireland Awards

Churchtown Renewal Trust, Co. Cork

Clare County Council

CLASP, County Library, Ennis

eircom Ennis Information Age Town Ltd.

Ennis Urban District Council

First Active PLC

Irish Life PLC

McMahon Group Property Services (est. 1900)

National Millennium Committee

Rural Resource Development Ltd.

Shannon Development Co.

St Joseph's Conference (Society of St Vincent de Paul)

Shoot the Scattering Trust Limited also acknowledges the valuable contributions of:

Dominic Considine and Ger Naughton
Special Edition sales

Ciana Campbell
Publicity

[10]

IRELAND
*A National Millennium
Committee Project*

Chairman's Foreword

One sunny Sunday morning almost three years ago my wife Mary and I were walking on the beach at Fanore in North Clare. With the wide Atlantic on one side and the stony Burren hills on the other, I was suddenly struck by the beauty of it all.

Then it occurred to me how heartbreaking it must have been for people to have to leave all this behind, crossing the ocean to a strange country to make a new life. And I wondered at that moment how many Clare people in exile were wishing they were back here now, on this bright blue Sunday morning.
I imagined that, for many, the pain of emigration must have been worse than a death in the family both for those who left and those who stayed behind. I felt we'd forgotten them. That was when I knew that something should be done to acknowledge the emigrant experience, to create a record that would endure as a testimony to the thousands of Clare people scattered around the world.
This book is the result.

From the start 'The Scattering' project has been marked by a generosity of energy and spirit from many people: the six photographers who travelled the world on their own time; the Clare people on every continent who welcomed them with open arms; the project team back at home who worked consistently on a voluntary basis to make this publication a reality.

We owe a particular debt to Dr. Patrick Hillery who supported our work from the beginning and accepted the invitation to be our Patron. We have had the benefit of his reputation and ability to achieve results quietly and effectively. His experience as a family doctor, public representative, Government Minister, European Commissioner and President of Ireland helped open many doors for us.

It is fitting that proceeds from this book will go to a charity whose aim it is to help the less well off. We have to remember that many of those who left Clare to seek their fortune, never found it. This book is for and about all Clare emigrants, those who made it and those who didn't.

We hope that through its publication we can, at least in spirit, welcome them all back home.

Dermot McMahon

Dermot McMahon
Chairman, Shoot the Scattering Trust Limited

Subscribers to The Scattering Special Edition

Aer Rianta, Shannon, Co. Clare

Allied Irish Bank, Bank Place, Ennis, Co. Clare

Bank of Ireland, Bank Place, Ennis, Co. Clare

Fr. Harry Bohan, Director, Rural Resource Development,
Town Hall, Shannon, Co. Clare

Thomas Barrett, Ard-Na-Gréine, Ennis, Co.Clare

Padraic Burke, Lowstrand Co., Lower Abbeygate Street, Galway

Shirley & Lauren Butler-Barrett, Gort-na Rí, Ennis, Co.Clare

Joe Casey, Main Street, Miltown Malbay, Co. Clare

John Casey & Co., Solicitors, Bindon Street, Ennis, Co. Clare

Mary Cashin, Solicitor, Francis Street, Ennis, Co. Clare

Churchtown Renewal Trust, Mallow, Co. Cork

Clare County Council, New Road, Ennis, Co. Clare

Clare County Library, Mill Road, Ennis, Co. Clare

Susan Clark, Moat Farm, Peasenhall, Saxmundham, Suffolk, England

Br. Matthias Comyns, Presentation College, St George's, Grenada, West Indies

Noel Connellan, Auditors & Accountants, Station Road, Ennis, Co. Clare

Michael Connolly, PO Box 911, Gaborone, Botswana, Africa

Cork City Library, Grand Parade, Cork

Cork County Library, Farranlea Road, Cork

County Clare VEC, Station Road, Ennis, Co. Clare

Geraldine Creaner, 43 D, Nova Court, Carrigaline, Co. Cork

Síle de Valera, Minister for Arts, Heritage, Gaeltacht & The Islands,
43/49 Mespil Road, Dublin 4

John Dilger, 17 Kingsley Street, Greylynn, Auckland, New Zealand

Peter & Patricia Dillon, Mountrivers, Doonbeg, Co. Clare

Donegal County Library, Rosemount, Letterkenny, Co.Donegal

Dromoland Castle Hotel, Newmarket-on-Fergus, Co. Clare

Joseph & Eileen Dundon, Coole, Castleconnell, Co. Limerick

Ennis Chamber of Commerce, 54 O'Connell Street, Ennis, Co. Clare

eircom Ennis Information Age Town, Quin Road Business Park, Ennis, Co. Clare

Mark FitzGerald, Sherry FitzGerald plc, Ormonde House, 12/13 Lower Leeson Street, Dublin

Steve Fitzgerald, 3 Edgewood Drive, Katonah, New York 10536, USA

Senan Fitzmartin, 4580 Staten Island Court, Plano, Texas 75024, USA

Alan Flynn, Old Ground Hotel, Ennis, Co. Clare

Paul Flynn, Ennis Electrical Supplies Ltd, 71a Parnell Street, Ennis, Co.Clare

Patricia Frawley, Curraghmore, Killaloe, Co. Clare

Dr. Gregory & Mrs. Anne Fried, 2 Effron Place, Great Neck, New York &
Cloonfeaghra, Corofin, Co. Clare

John Galvin, Clare Champion Ltd, Barrack Street, Ennis, Co. Clare

Galway County Library, Island House, Cathedral Square, Galway

Martin Hansbury, O'Sullivan & Hansbury Motors Ltd, Kilrush Road,
Ennis, Co. Clare

Sr. Canice Hanrahan, Mercy Education Office, Mungret College, Limerick

James Hardiman Library, National University of Ireland, Galway

Donald, Síofra, Cara Íosa & Lara Harrington, 4 Adelaide Terrace,
Glenageary, Co. Dublin

Kilrush Urban District Council, Kilrush, Co. Clare

Drs. Frank & Patricia Hassett, 19 Abbey Street, Ennis, Co. Clare

J. & F. Hegarty Property Ltd, Lifford, Ennis, Co. Clare

Seán Hegarty, 36 Grange Road, Rathfarnham, Dublin 14

Desmond J. Houlihan & Co. Solicitors, Salthouse Lane, Ennis, Co. Clare

Michael P. Houlihan, Solicitor, 9-11 Bindon Street, Ennis, Co. Clare

Caimin Jones, Blean, Kildysart, Co. Clare

Eamon Keane, Public Auditor & Accountant, Francis Street, Ennis, Co. Clare

Fr. Vincent Kelly, Fort Lauderdale, Florida, USA

Kerry County Library, Moyderwell, Tralee, Co. Kerry

Kildare County Library, Athgarvan Road, Newbridge, Co. Kildare

Frederick & Pauline Kirk, Kilmihil, Co. Clare

Ann Lawlor-MacNamara, Corbally, Quin, Co. Clare

Leitrim County Library, Ballinamore, Co. Leitrim

Limerick County Library, 58 O'Connell Street, Limerick

Limerick City Library, The Granary, Michael Street, Limerick

Martin Lynch, Clune Lynch & Co., Auditors & Accountants, 50 O'Connell Street, Ennis, Co. Clare

Angela Lyne, Queen's Hotel, Ennis, Co. Clare

Michael McDonagh, 59 Marian Avenue, Ennis, Co. Clare

Joe & Joan McDonnell, 16 Castlelawn, Ennis, Co. Clare

Dell McHugh, College Green, Ennis, Co. Clare

Brian M. McMahon, Solicitor, Parsons House, Woodquay, Ennis, Co. Clare

Niall McMahon, Cahercalla, Ennis, Co. Clare

McNamara Builders & Co. Ltd, Lisdoonvarna, Co. Clare

John & Vera Madden, Templegate Hotel, Ennis, Co. Clare

Marie Malone, 38 Ivy Hill, Gort Road, Ennis, Co. Clare

Mangan Brothers Ltd, Ashline, Kilrush Road, Ennis, Co. Clare

Patrick & Teresa Manning, 'White Gables', Keevagh, Quin, Co. Clare

Tom Mannion Travel, Worldchoice, Ennis, Co. Clare

Mayo County Library, Mountain View, Castlebar, Co. Mayo

Meath County Library, Railway Street, Navan, Co. Meath

Paddy & Marie Molony, 11 Kincora Park, Ennis, Co. Clare

Anthony Moore, TM Office Supplies, 43 Parnell Street, Ennis, Co.Clare

Mary Morrissey, 1 St. Flannan's Avenue, Clarecastle, Co. Clare

Marty Morrissey, RTE Sports, Donnybrook, Dublin 4

John & Bridie Mulcaire, 31 St. Senan's Road, Ennis, Co. Clare

Nano Murphy, Cahermurphy, Kilmihil, Co. Clare

Joe & Anne Noonan, Knockbeha, Caher, Co. Clare

Maisie O'Brien, Carrygerry, Newmarket-on-Fergus, Co. Clare

Sr. Mary O'Connell, Convent of Mercy, Kilkee, Co. Clare

Michael O'Dea, 62 Mountjoy Square, Dublin 1

Frances O'Neill, Kilrush/Dublin

Dr. Brendan O'Regan, The Bungalow, Newmarket-on-Fergus, Co. Clare

Philip O'Reilly & Co. Ltd, 22–24 Abbey Street, Ennis, Co. Clare

Frances O'Sullivan, Lissane, Clarecastle, Co.Clare

PricewaterhouseCoopers, Gardner House, Bank Place, Limerick

Eileen Reape, Moat Farm, Peasenhall, Saxmundham, Suffolk, England

Roche Ireland Ltd, Clarecastle, Co. Clare

Roscommon County Library, Abbey Street, Roscommon

Annette Ryan, PO Box 116, Freshwater 4870, Cairns, North Queensland, Australia

Ethel Ryan, Monivea Road, Ballybritt, Galway

Fr. Paul Ryan, Cloughleigh, Ennis

St. Flannan's College, Ennis, Co. Clare

Shannon Development, Shannon Town Centre, Shannon, Co. Clare

Fr. Patrick J. Sheils, St Anne's Church, Hans Bogbinders Alle 2, Copenhagen 230S Denmark

T. Sheils & Co., Gort Road, Ennis, Co. Clare

Philip Sherry, Sherry FitzGerald Countrywide, Ormonde House, 12–13 Lower Leeson Street, Dublin 2

Austin Slattery, Public Auditor & Accountant, Springfield Court, Ennis, Co. Clare

South Dublin Library, Unit 1, Belgard Square, Tallaght, Dublin 24

St. Columban's Library, Navan, Co. Meath

Mary Sweeney, Trócaire, 169 Booterstown Avenue, Co. Dublin

Valerie Sweeney, 16 Gleann na Smól, Shannon, Co. Clare

Senator Madeline Taylor-Quinn, Francis Street, Kilrush, Co Clare

Andy Tierney, Tierney's Office Automation, 8A Tracklands Business Park, Ennis, Co. Clare

Tipperary Joint Libraries Committee, Castle Avenue, Thurles, Co. Tipperary

Michael Vaughan, 42 Abbey Street, Ennis, Co. Clare

Bishop William Walshe, Westbourne, Ennis, Co. Clare

Waterford County Library, Library Headquarters, Lismore, Co. Waterford

Production Team

Anne Jones, Editor, is a graduate of University College Cork and worked as a teacher for several years before pursuing a career in public relations and radio. A former Controller of Programmes with Clare FM, she now works in media and communications.

Ray Conway, Writer, is a graduate in Law and Politics from University College Galway. A former producer with Clare FM, he has worked as a communications consultant and has written, produced and directed for theatre, film, video and radio.

Patricia Hanna, Project Co-ordinator, is a graduate of Trinity College, Dublin, Queen's University Belfast and the University of Ulster. In 1990 she moved to Ennis with her husband Bob and three children. She and Bob share ordained ministry and active involvement in local community life.

Anne Jones

Ray Conway

Patricia Hanna

Editor's Preface

Just as thousands of emigrants left their homes in Clare over the years, uncertain of what lay ahead of them, so we set out on our own journey almost three years ago to document the experience of some of them in what we hoped would be a meaningful and enduring way.

Enlisting the talents of some of the region's top photographers, we aimed to capture the diverse emigrant experience of one Irish county in a unique book of photographs to be published in the millennium year. What began as a simple wish to acknowledge the Clare Diaspora soon assumed a wider and deeper significance. It quickly became clear that this would be more than simply a book of pictures.

An open invitation was issued to the people of Clare to nominate friends or relations around the world for inclusion in the book. Irish embassies were contacted with details, as were religious orders, multinational companies and aid agencies. Wherever Clare people gathered, on whatever continent, we spread the word. The response was amazing. Nominations came pouring in from all over the county and around the world. With hundreds of names and addresses spanning four continents, the difficult task of selection began.

Finally, more than sixty subjects were chosen to be photographed. There were many hurdles. Time zones and borders, currencies and languages, tropical diseases and war zones, would all present their own unique challenges.

Over a twelve-month period the photographers criss-crossed the globe visiting Clare people at their work and in their homes. They found them in London and Seoul, Copenhagen and Chicago, in the outback of Australia and the African bush. Clare people were located in Poland, Papua New Guinea, Cyprus, Israel, Saudi Arabia, Nairobi, Nashville, New York, Pakistan, the Philippines, Paris, New Zealand, Madrid, Milan, the Lebanon.

The list of locations where Clare exiles have settled is long but each person in his or her own way is characteristic of the times they lived in, each reflecting a specific phase of a century of emigration. The young girls leaving for domestic service in the 1920s were followed by others fleeing the deprivations of the Economic War a decade later. The lure of plentiful work in the factories of wartime Britain was followed by the pitiful forced migration of the 1950s.

Significantly, too, the huge wave of enthusiastic young religious, men and women, who, 'went on the missions' in the 1950s and 60s, were notable by their absence in the 1980s and 90s. The last two decades of the century tell their own story.

Those who left in large numbers in the 1980s now come home regularly on holidays. Some speak of moving back some time, but wonder if they can afford to.

Advances in communications technology and reduced travel time have redefined the notion of exile. The turnaround in the economy has meant that going or staying is now much more a matter of choice. Nonetheless, significant numbers of young people are still leaving Clare to live and work abroad. But now, rather than being driven by hunger or desperation they seem to be following some long-established subconscious tradition, a need to 'see the world', for 'change', to 'travel', all intending to return to Clare to settle. It seems that emigration is now so deeply rooted in our culture that going away for a while seems to form part of a rite of passage with the knowledge that there is something now worth coming home for.

But coming home wasn't always that easy. The expectation of success formed part of the invisible baggage that every emigrant took away and few came back on visits unless they could clearly demonstrate that they had 'made it'. This was one of our biggest challenges when putting the book together. Traditionally we have sought to celebrate the most visibly successful of our emigrants. Otherwise we have largely ignored them. From the start it became clear that this book would not be a celebration of success and achievement. Rather it would be an acknowledgement of the everyday lives of the many Clare people scattered around the world, whatever their occupation, social standing or annual income. Each story has its own unique value.

When the photography was complete the crucial task of selecting the prints for inclusion in the book began. We worked closely with each photographer to ensure that the selection made reflected what they felt best captured the spirit of each subject. The subjects were then invited to tell their own stories in their own words.

The six photographers between them returned with thousands of images. But they brought back something else. Stories of a warm Clare welcome wherever they went, of a generosity of spirit and an openness that made a demanding job a little easier. What lingered longest in their memories, though, was the gratitude and wonder of the older emigrants that somebody had taken the time and trouble to travel halfway around the world to see them, to acknowledge their life's work, their effort and contribution and to know that they hadn't been forgotten.

This book isn't just about the Clare emigrants featured in its pages. It is about the shared experiences of emigrants everywhere, at all times and of all ages. For Clare people, of course, it will have a special significance. Emigration has been such a defining force in the culture of our county that none of us has gone untouched. When we look at these pages we see sons and daughters, brothers and sisters, aunts and uncles, cousins and friends.

And, if we take a closer look, we will see ourselves.

Anne Jones
Editor

The Photographers

John Kelly is a staff photographer with *The Clare Champion*. Completely self taught, to date he has won five National Media Awards, two Eircell Press Photographers' Association of Ireland Awards, the McNamee GAA Sports Photographer of the Year 1997 and the EBS Millennium Photography Competition.

Patrick McHugh is a graduate of the School of Visual Arts and Parsons School of Art and Design, New York. He has worked extensively in Europe and the USA on advertising and fashion campaigns for many agencies and magazines. He is now based in New York.

Christy McNamara is the recipient of the prestigious Communications Arts Award USA. He has exhibited widely in Europe, the UK, Scandinavia and North America. His book *The Living Note–The Heartbeat of Irish Music,* with Peter Woods, combines his two great loves–playing music and taking pictures.

Mike Mulcaire is self taught in the art of photography. His work has been exhibited in Ireland, the USA and Australia and has also featured in magazines, corporate campaigns and several album covers and is currently available in a series of postcards.

Veronica Nicholson is a graduate of the Dublin Institute of Technology; she has lectured at the Dún Laoghaire College of Art & Design and the Burren College of Art. Recent exhibitions include 'EV+A 2000', Limerick; 'Sheela -na-gig: In Search of the Walled Woman' at 1 Space Gallery, Chicago and the Pusan International Contemporary Art Festival in Korea.

Eamon Ward is a graduate of the Dún Laoghaire College of Art & Design. He was the Sunday Tribune/RTE Young Press Photographer of the Year in 1991. Other achievements include McNamee Best Sports Photographer of the Year Award and three Press Photographers Association of Ireland awards. He is a staff photographer with *The Clare Champion*.

John Kelly   Patrick McHugh   Christy McNamara   Mike Mulcaire   Veronica Nicholson   Eamon Ward

Emigration—An Enduring Tradition

The Irish, like many island peoples, have long been migrants. Irish monks established monasteries across Europe in early medieval times, and Irish invaders settled in western Scotland, bringing their language and customs with them. Irishmen have served at all levels in virtually every major European army. Irish religious of all denominations have left their mark on the presidents and peoples of countries as diverse as Zimbabwe, Lebanon, the Philippines, Chile and Nigeria. Irish scientists and engineers have designed and built public works in India, Africa and the Middle East. The Irish have been slave-traders in Nantes, wine-merchants in Bordeaux and Cadiz, fishermen in Newfoundland, farmers in Argentina.

The Famine was and remains the great watershed. It had such a cataclysmic impact on Irish society that its psychological and social effects are still to be felt. Not only did a million die and a further million flee the country, but it confirmed a tradition of departure which bled the country, generation after generation, of so many of its young people that Irish demography for that period constituted a unique case in the world. By the 1850s, New York was the third largest Irish city. Between the Famine and the 1950s, more than six million people left Ireland for good.

Referring to the 1930s, the *Reports of the Commission on Emigration and Other Population Problems* (1948–54) points out that of girls aged 10–14 in the Twenty-Six Counties in 1936, about 36 per cent, more than one-third, would end their lives outside the country. The corresponding figure for boys was 25 per cent.

The Reverend A. A. Luce, in his Reservation to the Commission's Report, put it bleakly:

'The hard core of the problem is the sad stark fact that one Irish child (more than one, statistically) in every three is born to emigrate, and grows up in the knowledge that he or she must emigrate. The moral and psychological effect of that fact is immense. It paralyses certain areas. It is a dead weight upon the spirit of the whole country, a dead hand upon her economy.'

[18]

The Denial of Emigration

Although born in New York and brought up in Limerick, Eamon de Valera was surely Clare's most famous political representative. His well-known broadcast on St Patrick's Day, 1943, began as follows:

'Before the present war began I was accustomed on St Patrick's Day to speak to our kinsfolk in foreign lands, particularly those in the United States, and to tell them year by year of the progress being made towards building up the Ireland of their dreams and ours—the Ireland that we believe is destined to play, by its example and its inspiration, a great part as a nation among the nations.

Acutely conscious though we all are of the misery and desolation in which the greater part of the world is plunged, let us turn aside for a moment to that ideal Ireland that we would have. That Ireland which we dreamed of would be the home of a people who valued material wealth only as a basis of right living, of a people who were satisfied with frugal comfort and devoted their leisure to the things of the spirit—a land whose countryside would be bright with cosy homesteads, whose fields and villages would be joyous with the sounds of industry, with the romping of sturdy children, the contests of athletic youths and the laughter of comely maidens, whose firesides would be forums for the wisdom of serene old age. It would, in a word, be the home of a people living the life that God desires that man should live.'

De Valera's attitude to emigration, and that of most of his generation, is instructive. As his opening words indicate, a ritual reference to emigrants was customary, in the same way as a ritual *cúpla focal* served for many decades instead of an effective language policy. Yet the reality was that millions left a place which could not offer them a future, and that the athletic youths and comely maidens were more likely to be encountered in Kilburn or Brooklyn than back at home.

In some parts of Ireland, the devastation wrought by emigration was such that houses were closed and shuttered as whole families left. In such cases it was the custom to bring the last burning embers from the hearth to a neighbour's house. Firesides, far from being cosy and serene, fell cold and silent. Rural Ireland became a place of ghosts and derelict buildings.

In the days of British rule there was the convenient explanation that maladministration and deliberate underdevelopment were the root causes of Ireland's chronic emigration. Later, when matters did not improve with independence, explanations were harder to come by. Perhaps it is not surprising, therefore, that the uncomfortable reality of continuing emigration in Ireland led to various kinds of denial. Emigration was a daily and painful reality experienced by almost every family and community in rural Ireland and by many, especially among the poor, in Ireland's towns and cities. Yet those who governed the country, for the most part, did little to alleviate it. Perhaps the fact that most of them were from backgrounds where emigration took a far lighter toll goes some way to explain this. Perhaps full employment and the end of emigration, like the restoration of the language, national re-unification and eternal salvation, were seen as projects so impossibly remote that ritual evocation, not action, sufficed for the present.

On the other hand, it would be easy to rush to judgement about the attitudes of de Valera and many of his contemporaries. It is true that policy at the time was naturally conservative, but we should remember the backdrop of a newly independent country experiencing a level of sheer grinding poverty that few in Ireland can now imagine. It should also be pointed out that there were some who were much more cold-blooded. For these people, continuing emigration was positively desirable: it removed the dangers of social unrest and guaranteed that the Irish middle classes could continue to live in the state to which they had become accustomed. It could even be presented as a positive good, with the export of so many fervent Catholics to far-off climes. Alexis Fitzgerald, in his Reservation to the Commission's Report, put it thus:

"I cannot accept either the view that a high rate of emigration is necessarily a sign of national decline or that policy should be over-anxiously framed to reduce it. It is clear that in the history of the Church, the role of Irish emigrants has been significant. If the historical operation of emigration has been providential, Providence may in the future have a similar vocation for the nation. In the order of values, it seems more important to preserve and improve the quality of Irish life and thereby the purity of that message which our people have communicated to the world than it is to reduce the numbers of Irish emigrants. While there is a danger of complacency I believe that there should be a more realistic appreciation of the advantages of emigration. High emigration, granted a population excess, releases social tensions which would otherwise explode and makes possible a stability of manners and customs which would otherwise be the subject of radical change. It is a national advantage that it is easy for emigrants to establish their lives in other parts of the world not merely from the point of view of the Irish society they leave behind but from the point of view of the individuals concerned whose horizon of opportunity is widened."

The Long-Term Effects of Emigration

The long-term effects of emigration on such a scale can only have been negative for the country. The *Commission on Emigration* notes the separation of children from their parents, of fathers from their families and of husbands from their wives, and the fact that many people, born in this country and whose natural inclination was to remain here, were forced by circumstances to leave it. No less real, but even more difficult to calculate, was the psychological effect of growing up in a country with few opportunities and less hope, where inheriting a farm or getting a permanent job were all-important, and where a prevailing inward-looking ethos and begrudgery ensured early change was not likely.

It is probably difficult for the Celtic Tiger generation fully to grasp this picture. Yet, as recently as the 1980s, a new wave of Irish emigrants left a depressed and debt-ridden country. In 1989 alone, 70,600 people left. Many became illegal immigrants in the US, leading to the rather extraordinary spectacle of the Government of Ireland lobbying the US Government in Washington to regularise the status of tens of thousands of Irish citizens for whom Ireland itself had no jobs.

Meanwhile, in the mid-1980s, the IDA had mounted a prominent, if unfortunately timed, campaign designed to attract foreign investment to Ireland by emphasising its young and highly qualified workforce. It featured a final year class of bright-eyed young UCD undergraduates, under the slogan 'The Young Europeans'. An investigative newspaper report some years afterwards found that the vast majority of those featured in the campaign had themselves emigrated.

We were told that we had a 'different class of emigrant' now: better educated and riding the crest of the transnational wave, acquiring valuable skills and experience before returning to Ireland. In the words of Brian Lenihan, in a notorious interview given to *Newsweek* magazine in October 1987, 'after all, we can't all live on a small island'. This flippant remark from a man of an otherwise sensitive and generous nature sparked an angry debate. After the heady days of 'joining Europe', free education and modernisation, it seemed as if we had jumped right back to the 1950s, a decade which few except the most perverse could wish to revisit. It is true that some well-qualified graduates were emigrating by choice and making good lives and careers in other places. Moreover, many have since returned and have greatly benefited Irish society and the Irish economy. But there were many others who would not have left if there had been greater opportunity at home; they were disproportionately drawn from marginal or poor communities and places. In part it always has been a matter of class. Those who ruled were not those who left or, if they did, it was by choice.

Emigrants, like all of us, made their own choices, although not in circumstances of their own choosing. It would be a mistake simply to present them as victims without agency of their own. Most went on to achieve fulfilled lives and to make an enormous contribution to other countries and other cultures. Emigration of the scale on which we experienced it gave Ireland a significance abroad out of all proportion to the size of the home population and the home country. Our loss was often someone else's gain. Moreover, many of those who left found opportunity, variety and fulfilment of a kind which would simply not have been possible had they remained at home. The lives of many such persons are portrayed in this book.

Clare Emigration

'I am to inform you that I received you welcomed letter on the 25th March dated January the 1st 55 which gave me and my Sister an ocean of consolation to hear that you my stepmother Brothers and Sisters are in good health thank God . . ." [grammar and spelling as in original]

Michael Normile, Lochinvar, Australia, letter written in 1855 to his father Michael at Derry, Liscannor
(from David Fitzpatrick's *Oceans of Consolation*: *Personal Accounts of Irish Migration to Australia*)
(1994) Cork University Press

Clare fulfilled all the conditions for a classic high-emigration county—heavy density of rural population, low valuation of agricultural land per head, high percentage of population living in rural areas and high percentage of agricultural areas in smallholdings. The Famine hit the county particularly hard and the subsequent pattern of high emigration was typical of Clare and all of the western seaboard Irish counties for more than a century.

From the Famine to the fifties Clare was always one of the top ten counties for the most rapid fall in population. In 1841, the population of the county stood at 286,394. Forty years later, in 1881, it was less than half that figure, 141,457. By 1951 it was only 81,329, and it fell further in the subsequent decade.

By the late 1940s, the average age on marriage in Clare was twenty-nine for a woman, thirty-four for a man. The really striking factor, however, was the marriage rate. Ireland had the lowest marriage rate in the world, at about five persons per thousand per annum, at that time. Other European countries, and the USA, had rates of over twice this level. Within Ireland, Clare consistently had one of the lowest marriage rates of any county between 1910 and 1947. One can thus conclude that for most of the first half of the twentieth century Clare had one of the lowest rates of marriage anywhere in the world, an ironic posthumous vindication of Brian Merriman's caustic comments in *Cúirt an Mheánoíche*. When couples did marry, of course, they had large families, but as we have seen earlier, many of these children would subsequently emigrate. Any natural increase in the population was always more than outweighed by emigration, perpetuating a long-term pattern of decline. In the 1946–51 period, the five counties with the highest rates of emigration per thousand population were (in descending order) Leitrim, Kerry, Clare, Roscommon and Cavan.

Today the trend has halted; the present population of the county stands at just fewer than 90,000. Indeed, the census of 1996 records a 10.4 per cent increase in only five years in the population of Ennis, from 16,058 to 17,726, compared to 1991. Clare and the mid-West region are now experiencing a growing demand for employment and an inward flow of population, replacing the long-term pattern of constant outward migration.

A Strong Culture of Emigration

'I thought I stooped to kiss her as in the days of yore
Says she "Mike you're only joking as you often were before"
The cock crew on the roost again, he crew both loud and shrill
And I awoke in California, far far from Spancilhill'

From the original version of *Spancilhill* as collected by Robbie McMahon, composed in California by Michael Considine in the late nineteenth century.

The American historian Kerby Miller, writing about Irish emigration, distinguished between 'emigrants' and 'exiles'. Exiles defined themselves by reference to their native land and looked constantly to the past. Emigrants were a more forward-looking lot and thought of themselves in terms of their adopted land, not the one they had left. Irish people, he suggested, were strongly attached to their native places and to the pre-modern world-view embodied in their culture.

The reality is more complex. There is really no necessary contradiction between the retention of a strong if sometimes sentimental attachment to the home place while forging a new life elsewhere; indeed the one may sometimes be the prerequisite of the other. One of the places where these contradictions are most clearly played out is in the music and folklore of the people. 'Spancilhill' and *'Bánchnoic Éireann Óighe'* have become, in their own quite different ways, anthems of emigration and exile.

[21]

Beir beannacht óm chroí go Tír na hÉireann
Bánchnoic Éireann Óighe
Chun a mhaireann de shíolrach Ír is Éibhir
Ar bhánchnoic Éireann Óighe
An áit úd in arbh aoibhinn binnghuth éan
Mar shámhchruit chaoin ag caoineadh Gael
Is é mo chás bheith míle míle i gcéin
Ó bhánchnoic Éireann Óighe
Is fairsing is is mór iad cruacha Éireann
Bánchnoic Éireann Óighe
A cuid meala agus uachtar ag gluaiseacht ina slaoda
Ar bhánchnoic Éireann Óighe
Rachaidh mé ar cuairt, nó is luath mo shaol
Don talamh bheag shuairc is dual do Ghaeil,
Is gur fearr liom ná duais dá uaisleacht é
Bheith ar bhánchnoic Éireann Óighe

Donnchadh Rua Mac Conmara, Cratloe, 1715–1810, probably written in Hamburg, Germany.

While this book is an acknowledgement of the lives of a modest number of current Clare emigrants, their predecessors have made varied, significant and colourful contributions to many other countries. Even a few names convey a sense of the range of people and places involved.

Thomas O'Gorman, Castletown, 1732–1809 became a soldier and wine-merchant in France. James Bartholomew Blackwell, Ennis, 1763–1820, French republican and reputed stormer of the Bastille, was a member of Hoche's ill-fated Bantry Bay expedition and later served with Napoléon in Prussia and Austria. Joseph Kavanagh, born in Lille, of Clare descent, was also a revolutionary republican and the subject of a contemporary pamphlet *Les exploits glorieux du célèbre Cavanagh. Cause première de la liberté française.* William Smith O'Brien of Dromoland, 1803–1864, was deported to Tasmania for his part in the 1848 rebellion. Charles James Mahon, Ennis, 1800–1891, politician and soldier, allegedly managed to serve with the armies of Russia, Turkey, Austria, Uruguay, Chile, Brazil and the USA; he was certainly one of the last of the gentleman soldiers.

Hugh McCurtin, Kilmacreehy, Corcomroe, 1680–1755, poet and lexicographer, chronicler of the O'Briens, spent a significant part of his life in France. Thomas Dermody, Ennis, 1775–1802, became a poet and soldier in England. William Mulready, Ennis, 1786–1863 was one of London's best-known society painters in his day. Harriet Smithson, Ennis, 1800–1854, singer, married Berlioz in Paris; his Symphonie Fantastique was composed in her honour. Frederick Burton, Corofin, 1816–1900, became a painter and Director of the English National Gallery. Edna O'Brien of Tuamgraney, one of the most acclaimed of modern Irish writers, is herself one of the subjects of this book.

Richard Barry O'Brien, Kilrush, 1847–1918, was a notable lawyer and author in London. Caitlín (MacNamara) Thomas, 1913–94, whose father was from Ennistymon, married the Welsh poet Dylan Thomas; it was a turbulent marriage.

Patrick Hannan, 1840–1925, discovered the Kalgoorlie goldmine in Australia in 1849. John Philip Holland, a former Christian Brother of Liscannor (1841–1914) invented the submarine. Originally intended as a possible offensive weapon against the British, it was subsequently taken up by the American Navy and the British Royal Navy.

Conclusion

Ireland, and Clare, are changing. Emigration is no longer a one-way trip, as final as the last voyage. If the 'American Wake' still exists, it is a relatively light-hearted affair. Frequent travel, cheap communications and the interlinkages of global culture have made the world a smaller place. Moreover, employment opportunities in most parts of Ireland, including Clare, have improved dramatically in recent years. If a person wishes nowadays to remain in Ireland rather than emigrate, it is much easier to do so. Many return after spending time abroad.

We are becoming a little more comfortable, and maybe a little more honest, with ourselves and with our past. With this change, public recognition of the Diaspora and their part in our own story is coming at last. In part this is the spirit of the age, in which migration in all its forms is increasingly recognised as a central part of the human experience. In part it is the role played by Presidents Patrick Hillery, Mary Robinson and Mary McAleese, all of whom have sought to reach beyond the territory of Ireland to the Irish community worldwide. In part it is because Irish migrants themselves are no longer prepared to remain silent and forgotten.

We should not be complacent. Not all of our emigrants have done well. It would be a doubly cruel blow if, having rejected them by obliging them to leave in the first place, a newly wealthy Ireland were to refuse to help them now. Some may wish to return; we should take steps to make this possible.

Meanwhile, we continue to deny our citizens abroad the right to vote—something which many other emigrant countries such as Italy and Poland have long granted their citizens. And if we do not create a more equal society here in Ireland, all of our wealth will not prevent the departure of those who continue to feel that there is no place for them at the table.

It is good to note that not all migrant traffic has been one-way. Clare has been ably served by two foreign-born political representatives, Éamon de Valera and Dr. Moosajee Bhamjee. Shannon Airport, as well as being the port of exit for generations of Irish emigrants, has also been the point of arrival for thousands of others, including the children and grandchildren of previous emigrants. In recent years, well before asylum-seekers and refugees became an issue in other parts of Ireland, Clare welcomed people who applied for asylum in Shannon and established an active and well-supported office of the Irish Refugee Council in Ennis.

There is a danger, with the present climate of progress and change in Ireland, that we may forget the sacrifices made by previous generations when he left, as well as the enormous contributions which they made to other places. But if we deny the reality of the Irish Diaspora, we deny a significant part of our own identity. This is especially important because of the rapid changes in Ireland itself. It is ironic that in some respects the emigrant Irish constitute one of the last repositories of an Irish cultural identity which has now all but disappeared in Ireland itself. If we are fully to respect and preserve this identity, we can begin by providing a space where the tales of those who left can be told.

Emigration is a phenomenon which we usually think about in the plural: the movement of people. However, we can only understand it in the singular: individual and unique decisions, experiences, stories.

That is why this book is so important.

Piaras Mac Éinrí
Stiúrthóir/Director
Ionad na hImirce/Irish Centre for Migration Studies
Ollscoil Náisiúnta na hÉireann, Corcaigh/National University of Ireland, Cork

Between the Mountains and the City
Anne Casey

Photographer John Kelly

Born in 1967, Anne Casey grew up in Miltown Malbay. After graduating
from University College Dublin she worked for a while in public
relations and publishing before backpacking across the USA and
finally ending up in Australia. After coming home briefly to Ireland
in 1994 she returned to Australia where she now lives.

'I've always wanted to travel. Maybe it had something to do with all the
colourful bedtime stories my parents told me. Growing up on the edge
of the Atlantic probably had something to do with it as well.

When I graduated from college I started working in Dublin as a corporate
public relations consultant and later moved into business magazine
publishing. But as my twenty-fifth birthday approached in 1992 I knew
I had to get out and see the world. So I left my job, promising to return,
and travelled via the USA to Sydney, Australia, armed with a working
holiday visa.

After living and working in Sydney for a while, I then travelled by "ute"
(that's Australian for pick-up truck) up through the centre of New South
Wales to the coast of Northern Queensland, then back down to Sydney
— about 8,000 kilometres. I left Australia in September 1993 and toured
New Zealand and South-East Asia before returning to my job in Dublin
early in 1994. But it was no good. I couldn't stay. By October I was on
the plane back to Sydney. I'd fallen in love with the golden beaches, the
fabulous forests and, of course, the glorious weather.

And this is where I've been ever since. I divide my time between the Blue
Mountains and the city where I work as National Director of
Communications, Tax and Legal Services for PricewaterhouseCoopers.

A hectic work life is balanced by weekends at the beach or in the
mountains, occasionally disturbed by the purring presence of a laptop
computer. I love nature and Australia still has plenty of unspoilt
vastness left to offer the explorer. After a busy time at the office some
yoga, or a walk in the woods, is still a great way to unwind.'

Out On His Own
Mark Naughton

Photographer John Kelly

Born in 1969, Mark Naughton grew up in Kilkee. After spending some time in London he emigrated to New Zealand in 1993 where he now runs a successful business fitting out interiors. He is married with two children.

'When I was eighteen I went off to England and ended up staying with an aunt of mine in Gillingham. I worked in labouring, cladding underground stations for a Clareman, P. J. Linnane. Then I decided I needed to learn some skills so I did an electrician's course with City and Guilds. After a while I was getting bored with London and then I met a girl from New Zealand in a pub. That's how I ended up out here!

We moved out to Auckland in October 1993 and got married the following February. Now we have two girls aged five and three. I started working first for a man from Belfast but within a year I was out on my own doing interior fit-outs. You can do well here if you're prepared to work at it. It's all contract work, there's no hourly rate. You get paid for what you do and that's it.

Being Irish here has been a big advantage. Maybe it's that we have a better education but we seem to have an edge on most other people who come out here—a better understanding of the world and certainly we'd have far more general knowledge than most.

I don't miss the weather back home, that's for sure but I do miss the people. I'd go back tomorrow if I could but I've got a house here now, a young family and a business with a couple of guys working for me. I haven't been home to Clare since I came out to New Zealand. That's nearly seven years now. Maybe I'll get to make a trip back soon.'

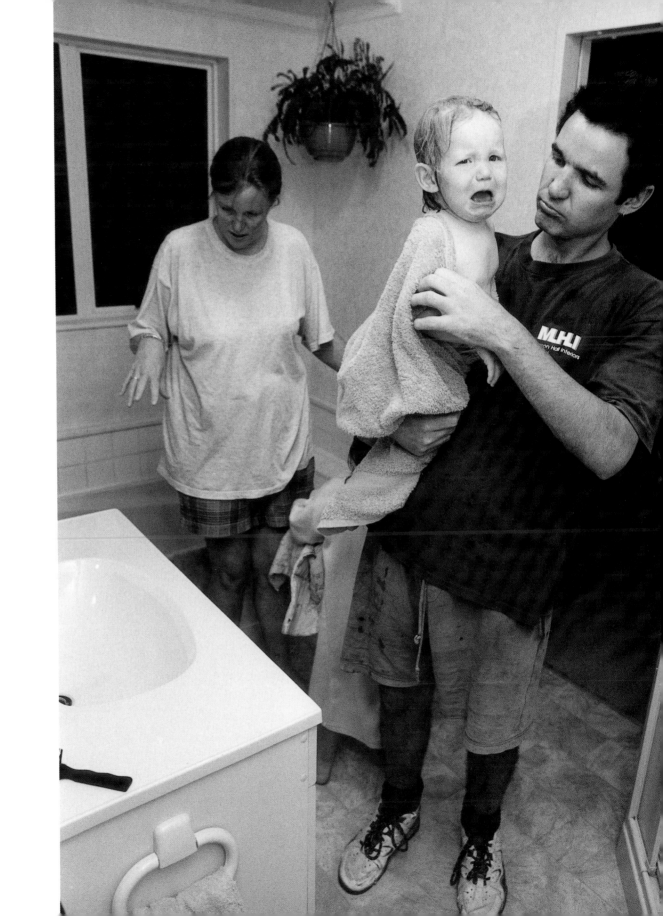

NYPD Blue
Michael Power

Photographer Patrick McHugh

Michael Power was born in 1966 and grew up in Barr-na-Gaoithe, Darragh. After leaving school he worked for a year in Dublin before going to New York. In 1987 he joined the NYPD and is now a Sergeant stationed in Manhattan.

'The first job I got in New York was as a toll collector on the Henry Hudson Bridge. It was horrible, breathing fumes all day and taking dog's abuse from stressed-out drivers. My aunt worked for the Police Department and she suggested I take the entrance exam. I did and passed it.

After six months at the New York City Police Academy I was sent to the 48th precinct in the South Bronx. After my probation I was sent to the 34th precinct in Washington Heights in Manhattan. This area had the highest murder rate in New York City, over a hundred homicides a year for one and a half square miles. Looking back now I guess it was probably a dangerous place to work. At the time I just went out and did my job. While I was there, three policemen from my precinct were killed on duty.

I was promoted to Sergeant in August of 1995 and transferred to the 20th precinct on the Upper West Side of Manhattan. That September I couldn't make it home so I found myself listening to the All-Ireland Final in the patrol car. My partner for that day was an African-American officer, Keith Johnson. He drove on quietly as his Sergeant jumped around and roared at the radio. When Clare won the game I went crazy. Then I noticed Keith was looking at me a little strangely. I didn't know whether to hit him or hug him. I don't think he could fully grasp the global significance of the event.

I return to Clare as often as I can. I may retire to Darragh, if I can afford to live in the Celtic Tiger economy. Things have changed a lot at home since I left. The people are the same though, and that's what really counts.'

Mercy Mission
Mary Elizabeth McNamara

Photographer Eamon Ward

Sr. Loretto McNamara was born in Crusheen in 1934. After school she joined the Mercy Sisters and taught for many years before becoming the Principal at Coláiste Muire in Ennis. In 1989 she went to Kenya where she has lived and worked since.

'After my profession I spent some time teaching in Spanish Point and then many, many years in Coláiste Muire, Ennis, as a teacher and in administration. One of the most memorable events, while I was running the school, was my daring feat of successfully overtaking the squad car at a very high speed to net one of my mitching students!

I took early retirement in 1989 and volunteered for a teaching apostolate with our Mercy Sisters in Kenya. I'm stationed in the little village of Nguutani near Mwingi which is north of Nairobi.

The area is semi-arid and very impoverished and so our work is aimed at encouraging self-sufficiency for the people here. We run a commercial college for girls, teaching them secretarial and sewing skills. None of this would be possible without the generous assistance we get from our many friends back in Ireland and especially Clare.

At the moment we're experiencing the worst famine in over sixty years. AIDS has reached epidemic proportions here and orphans are everywhere. The poor cannot afford even one meal a day and many are dying from malnutrition. Violent robberies are on the increase and it is difficult to feel safe nowadays. If the Western powers cancelled Kenya's huge international debt we might see some improvement. As it is, the future looks bleak.

But it is still a beautiful country and it is a great honour and privilege to serve the people here.'

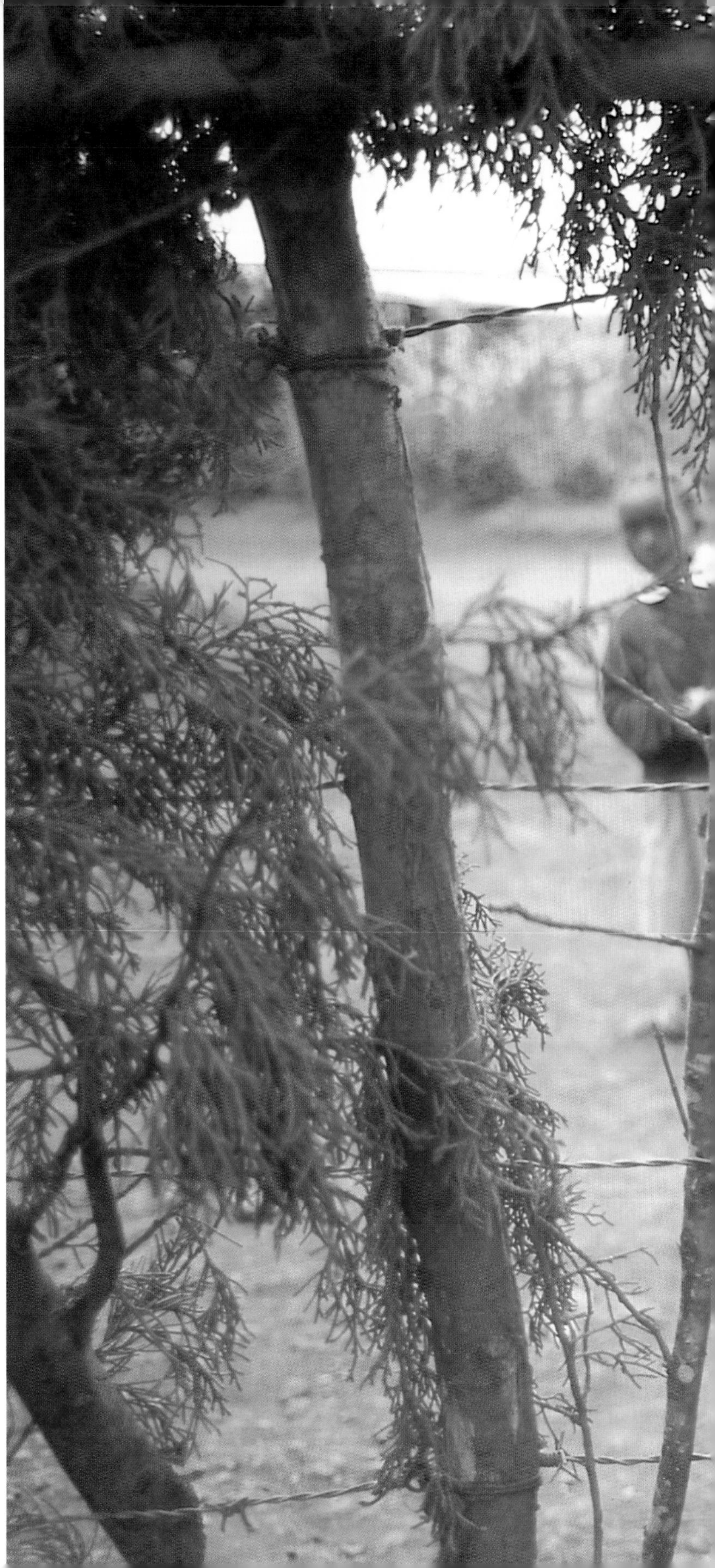

Labour of Love
Denis Dillon

Photographer Christy McNamara

Born in 1961, Denis Dillon grew up in Knocknageeha by the shores of Lough Graney. After graduating from the National Institute for Higher Education, Limerick, he emigrated to England in 1985. He now manages a training and education centre and is a Councillor for the London Borough of Haringay.

'The parish of Killanena-Flagmount is one of the most beautiful, unspoilt parts of Ireland and I think I'm very lucky to have grown up there. I went to Duglawn National School and for a while to the new Flagmount School when it opened. Then I went to Our Lady's College in Gort where I sat my Leaving Cert in 1979. After working for a few years I did a BA in European Studies at NIHE Limerick and graduated in 1985. Then, like tens and thousands of others at the time, I went to England in search of work.

For my first year in England I worked with the Department of Health and Social Security dealing with benefit claims. Since 1986 however, I have been working in the area of training and education, focussing specifically on the needs of disadvantaged young people and adults.

I currently work as a local centre manager for the Community Service Volunteers, a UK-wide charity that supports those who suffer disadvantage in relation to employment and learning opportunities.

For most of my time in London I have been active in Labour Party politics and in 1998 was elected as a Councillor for my local borough. I am currently a member of the Council's executive with specific responsibility for regeneration, economic development and social inclusion. I am also a member of the Labour Party's Irish Society which campaigns for the welfare of the Irish Community in Britain and for a just and lasting solution to the conflict in Northern Ireland.

I come home to Knocknageeha about three times a year and keep in touch with what is happening in Clare by way of a time honoured tradition—reading *The Clare Champion* every week.'

[41]

Hollywood Dreams
Blue McDonnell

Photographer Patrick McHugh

Rachel 'Blue' McDonnell was born in Ennis in 1965. After leaving school she trained as an embalmer. She then travelled around Europe before getting a job in the anatomy department of University College Cork. In 1994 she emigrated to the USA. After driving trucks for a year she took a course in theatre and drama and is now pursuing a career in acting in Los Angeles.

'I was fourteen years old when I told my mother I wanted to be an embalmer. My parents hoped it was a passing phase but I was determined to pursue my chosen trade. The summer of my Leaving Cert. I got a job with Fanagan's Funeral Directors in Dublin. The day I did my first embalming was the true beginning of my life with death!

I enrolled on a course at the College of Embalming in Birmingham and after graduating, worked in Germany and then at University College Cork. After a few years I decided it was time to hit the road again, and headed for the States.

I found myself in Texas where I got a job driving an 18-wheeler for Schneider National, a large trucking company and ended up working all over the States. I had a few hairy and scary experiences but I have to admit, it was pretty exciting.

After a year of trucking it was time to get down to what I really wanted to do—acting. I enrolled in a school of acting in Dallas and after I graduated, headed to Los Angeles.

For the business I'm in, it's the place to be but the acting work comes and goes. It's a feast or a famine. My agent and my manager claim that stardom is just around the corner. That's what I pay them to say anyway! In the meantime I'm doing odd jobs to keep the bread and peanut butter on the table. I live in Santa Monica, by the sea and the sun shines all the time, so in a profession that requires so much resting, I can't think of a better place to be.'

AIDS Priest
Bernard Lynch

Photographer Eamon Ward

Fr. Bernard Lynch grew up in Ennis in the 1950s. He was ordained as a member of the Society of African Missions in 1971 and the following year left for Africa. He was later assigned to New York City where he began ministry to the Gay and Lesbian Communities. Opposed by the Church authorities, he was the subject of a failed criminal prosecution. He now lives in London.

'After serving in Zambia for several years I was assigned to further studies in New York. While teaching in the North East Bronx I completed a master's degree in counselling psychology and a doctorate in theology and psychology. Around that time I was appointed theological consultant to the Board of Directors of Dignity New York, an organisation for Lesbian and Gay Catholics and their friends. When the AIDS epidemic hit in the early 1980s, I started an AIDS ministry programme and soon was drafted into the Mayor's Task Force on AIDS.

I campaigned for safer sex and testified before the City Council for civil rights legislation to protect the sick and dying from discrimination in jobs and housing. The Archdiocese of New York vehemently opposed such legislation, censured my work and ordererd me to Rome in 1987. A campaign was started against me culminating in accusations of abuse by a former student. After a media circus the prosecution case collapsed, as it became apparent that the evidence had been fabricated in order to end my outreach work with sexual minorities and people with AIDS.

The media coverage continued with an appearance on the *Late Late Show* in Ireland and three one-hour documentaries aired on Channel 4. In February 1993 Bloomsbury Press published my account of the events in my book *Priest On Trial*.

I now live in London and continue to work with people living with and affected by HIV-AIDS. I also have a private practice in psychotherapy. I have made several contributions to books written on spirituality and sexuality and am currently working on a theology of sexual liberation that I hope to have published next year.'

Handball Ace
Pat Kirby

Photographer Patrick McHugh

Pat Kirby was born in Tuamgraney in 1936. After working in Ennis for several years he emigrated to the USA in 1959. A legend in the world of handball, he is a former US, Irish and World Champion. He now lives in Tucson, Arizona.

'When I hit the streets of New York I felt totally lost. It seemed like a great big beehive to me with people running here and there like crazy. First I got a job with Reeves Stores, a grocery chain run by a man from Scariff and after a while I moved into construction.

In 1961 I was drafted into the army and was introduced to American handball. They played with a small hard ball on a smaller court and everyone wore gloves but I adjusted pretty quickly and ended up winning the army championships. After discharge, I joined the New York Athletic Club and in 1965 I won the US Senior and Junior National titles. In 1970 I represented the USA in the World Championships held in Dublin and won the World title. There was a big parade through Scariff and Tuamgraney to welcome home their new World Champion.

I'd married a Galway girl, Carrie Beckett, in 1964 and we have three daughters. In 1972 we moved back to Ireland and between 1974 and 1980 I won fifteen National Championships in both the small and big court. By then, though, we realised that there would be a better future for our girls in the States so we moved to Tucson in 1980.

I got a job as a carpenter in the university there and retired three years ago as a supervisor. I still continued to play handball and won the National Masters title twelve times straight. I was fifty-two years old when I won it last. In 1992 I had a hip replacement operation so I don't play any more. But when I look at all the medals and trophies around the house I suppose you could say I haven't done too badly for a country lad from Tuamgraney.'

In the Outback
Peggy Perrins

Photographer John Kelly

Peggy Perrins (née Downes) comes from Moveen near Kilkee. In the early 1970s she went to London where she met and married Peter Perrins. After spending some time in Africa they settled in Australia where they have lived for the past nineteen years. They have two grown-up sons.

'I remember one Christmas my uncle sent me a picture-book. There was a story in it about sheep farmers in Australia and it fascinated me. I used to look at the pictures and dream about going to Australia one day.

After I left school I went to Dublin and then to London where I got a job in a solicitor's office while working nights in a pub. That's where I met Peter. He was from Rhodesia, as it was then, and he was travelling the world. We got married in 1973 and when we decided to travel, there was only one place I wanted to see.

We bought a motorbike in Sydney, a Honda, and toured all the way up to Darwin. By that time I was expecting our first child, Clifford, and Peter wanted him born in Africa. So I found myself in Bulawayo working in an insurance office with a young child and another one on the way. Although we loved Africa, we began to think about the children's education and in 1981 we moved back to Australia.

After a while in Melbourne we headed up to Cairns and bought a block of land at Rockhampton. That's where we are now, miles from anywhere! It's very rural and quite rough and I think that's why I like it. I'm now working at an old folk's home as a nursing assistant and I love the job.

When I was growing up in Clare there were always horses on the farm and now I have some of my own. Sometimes when I'm out here with them I look around at the rolling hills and imagine I could be back in Clare—without the rain, of course!'

[53]

The Lonesome Touch
Martin Hayes

Photographer Patrick McHugh

Martin Hayes comes from Maghera, Feakle. He started playing the fiddle at an early age and joined the famous Tulla Céilí Band when he was thirteen. In 1985 he emigrated to the USA and now lives in Seattle. Widely recognised as one of the most talented fiddle players of his generation, Martin has four albums to his credit.

'For as long as I can remember, my father has been playing the fiddle and when I was seven he began to teach me. He bought me a half-sized fiddle for Christmas and he only ever taught me to play when I would ask him. I'd sit in front of him and mimic his movements and hum the music. Then I'd go into my room alone and practise the same way as other kids would belt a sliothar up against a gable wall.

My father had been a member of the Tulla Céilí Band since it was formed in the 1940s and when I was thirteen I joined it as well. The band played two nights a week, at halls all over the country, but they made it back home by dawn, whatever the distance, because everyone had a farm to look after. I remember going out for the cows at five in the morning, because there was early milking on a Sunday.

I moved to the USA in 1985. I had already toured the country with the Tulla Céilí Band so I wasn't a total stranger to the place. I started out in Chicago playing everything from rock and roll to blues and jazz. I experimented with a lot of different styles but found myself coming back again and again to the tunes that I had played with my father as a child.

In 1993 I moved to Seattle where I now live. I make my living as a touring musician, most of the time in the States but also travelling all over the world. Each year I return to Clare to play at the Willie Clancy Summer School, the Feakle Festival, in sessions at Pepper's pub and to play with the Tulla Band.

For me the message of music is always yearning to be expressed and yet it can never be totally expressed. No matter where you go in the world the essence of the music is always the same, all that changes is the style. For me now I wouldn't see much of a distinction between Micho Russell, Miles Davis and Bach.'

At the Heart of Europe
Frank Barrett

Photographer John Kelly

Frank Barrett grew up in Kildysart. A graduate of University College Galway, he was elected to Clare County Council in 1985. In 1989 he moved to Brussels to work for the European Parliament and has been there ever since. Frank is the son of former TD, Minister and MEP, Sylvester Barrett.

'When I left college in the mid-1970s there were very few opportunities for graduates. I eventually got a job with Tipperary County Council but Nenagh was too quiet and too far away from the sea for me. I left after two years and bought a fishing boat, working out of Kilbaha and Carrigaholt for a few years. Around this time I met my future wife, Nora Bugler, from Ennis and we were married in October 1983.

I've always had an interest in politics and worked for my father's campaign when he was elected an MEP for Munster in 1984. Then, in 1985, I was elected a Fianna Fáil County Councillor for the Ennis area. Our son Seán was born the same year. I stood for the Dáil in 1987 but didn't win a seat.

After that, I decided it was time to get back to making a living for my family. The job with the European Parliament came up in April 1989 and I resigned my council seat. We sold the fishing boat and moved to Brussels for what we thought would be a few years. Then our daughter Sarah was born, we bought a house, the kids started school and I kept getting promoted. At the moment I am Secretary General of the UEN (Union for Europe of the Nations) group in the Parliament which includes the Fianna Fáil MEPs.

We still plan to move back to Clare some time, we just don't know when that will be. Right now, Brussels is a good place for us so we'll probably stay here a few more years.

Some days, though, when the sun is beating down on the busy city outside my window I can think of nothing better than to be at the wheel of my fishing boat hitting out into the Atlantic off Carrigaholt.'

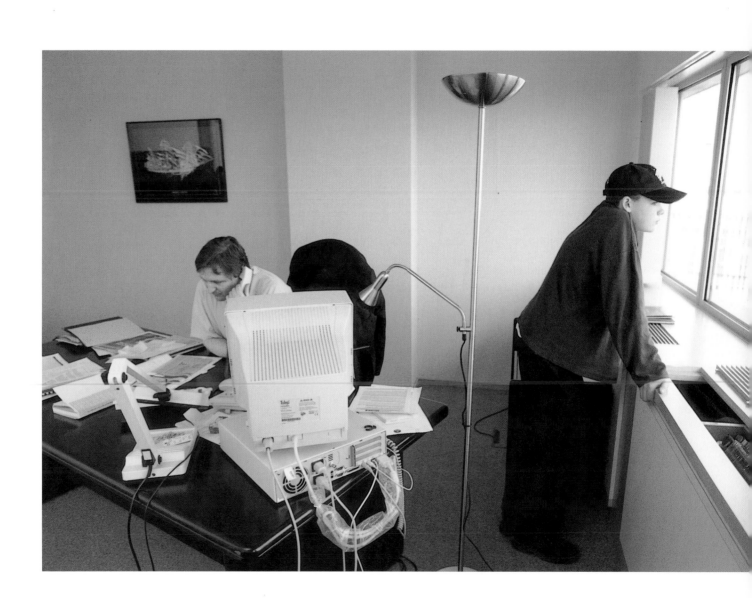

On the Westchester Line
John O'Halloran

Photographer Christy McNamara

John O'Halloran was born in Quin in 1955. He trained as a
carpenter and worked around Clare before emigrating to
New York in the mid-1980s where he now lives with his wife
and two children.

'I decided to go to the States in 1984. Things were bad in Ireland at
the time and people were emigrating in big numbers again. It wasn't
hunger that drove me out though. I think it was more for a bit of
adventure, to see what it was like on the other side.

When I arrived in New York I stayed with friends of mine in the
Bronx and the first day I went looking, I got a job. I started rigging
scaffolding, something I hadn't done a lot of back home but I liked
the work and I spent the next five years at it. Rigging is heavy work
and it's dangerous. We worked on a lot of high-rise buildings so you
had to have a great respect for heights. I loved the challenge of it
and worked on some great projects like the restoration of the Statue
of Liberty and Ellis Island.

I'd always wanted to do finished carpentry work and in the early
1990s I moved on to work in that area. Now, instead of working on
the outside of the high-rise buildings I work on the interiors installing
panels, doors and any other specialised woodwork that's required.
I married Susan Sigel in 1988 and we have two boys, Jake and
Daniel. We live out in Woodlawn, on the Westchester line. We get
home to Ireland twice a year, usually for a month in the summer with
the kids, then I come back for a week's shooting in November during
the Thanksgiving break.

People always say to me that I've never lost my Clare accent. Well, it
would be hard for me to lose it. All the companies I work for out here
are Irish and so is most of my neighbourhood. My kids don't have a
Clare accent but they have lots of my slang.'

La Dolce Vita
Mary Browne

Photographer Eamon Ward

Born in 1951, Mary Browne comes from the Circular Road in Ennis. Soon after leaving school she got a job with Aer Lingus. In the mid-1970s she moved to their office in Rome and later to Milan where she now lives and works.

'After I did my Leaving Cert I worked with the County Council for a few months and then I got a job with Aer Lingus in their reservations and ticketing office in Limerick. That was in April 1970. The job meant we got concessions on flights so, whenever we could, my friends and I took off. Once, when we were going to Amsterdam, our mothers shook holy water on us and told us not to talk to strangers. But we did. He was Italian, from Sicily actually, and three months later he turned up in Ireland with his twin brother. Eventually, my friend and I ended up marrying them!

In 1975 I was transferred to the Aer Lingus office in Rome. I fell in love with Italy straight away. I loved the Italians, the way they expressed themselves and I loved the way you could sit outside the cafés drinking coffee and never get wet. The following year, when I moved to Milan I bought a moped. I was slowly becoming Italian. I married Salvatore (Toto) in 1977 and now we have two teenage daughters Vanessa and Valeria. They say they are half Sicilian and half Irish.

I manage the Aer Lingus office here in Milan. Basically my job is to send Italians to Ireland. If I'm asked where in Ireland a visitor should go, I'll always recommend Clare. In Milan the summers are very hot and I miss being near the sea. But I don't get nostalgic about Clare. When you have a home and family it doesn't matter where you live, they still haven't reinvented the kitchen sink . . . it's the same wherever you are!'

You Leave in May
Paud Sheils

Photographer Veronica Nicholson

Fr. Patrick Sheils was born at the Friary Bow in Ennis in 1924. Although set to take over the family business, he joined the Redemptorist Order instead and was ordained to the priesthood in 1954. He spent many years in the Philippines and since 1978 he has been based in a parish in Copenhagen.

'After I was ordained I assumed I would be working for the missions in Ireland. Then one day I got a postcard from the Provincial in Limerick. It simply said: "You are hereby appointed to the Philippines. You leave in May".

I left for the Philippines in 1956 and I would never see my father alive again. A telegram came to the mission station. "Dad died in his sleep this morning". On the second round back to the Philippines, another telegram, this one informing me of my mother's death. At that time there was no possibility of getting home for the funerals.

In the Philippines I learned the language quickly enough and spent my first and happiest Christmas there at our leper colony in Cebu. We had much to teach the people by way of prayers, the Mass and the sacraments but they had a faith, kindness, patience, courage and a closeness to God which we could only envy.

1978 saw me back in Ireland giving missions around the country, mostly in Clare where I felt so much at home. Then came another message from our Provincial who asked me to go to Denmark for a month. Well, it's been a long month. I've been here now for twenty-two years and it has been the most challenging mission I could ever have imagined. Filipinos have come here to seek a better economic future. Once again I am surrounded by these kind and gentle people. They have a wonderfully rich culture, tradition and faith to share with us Europeans.

Just as we went out to help the poor and needy in other lands, I feel that people from these lands are now here among us to help restore to us what we have lost. We should welcome them.'

Island Exile
Nora Sullivan

Photographer Christy McNamara

Nora Sullivan (née Moran) was born on Scattery Island in 1919. When she was in her teens her family moved to the mainland and in the early 1940s Nora emigrated to England. She married in 1945 and moved to Swansea where she raised her family. Nora Sullivan died in May, 2000.

'We moved into Kilrush from the Island in the 1930s and it was from there that I headed off to work in England. There was plenty of work there during the war and I ended up in a sheet metal factory in the midlands. The job was tough and we worked away between air raids. I came home from work one day to find all my street gone. What could you do? You just carried on.

John Sullivan was a fireman in the RAF when I met him and after the war we got married and moved down to Swansea, his home town. In 1946 our first girl Margaret was born. Over the next few years Maureen and Angela followed and I stayed at home to raise them. Then the kids started going to grammar school. In those days education wasn't free and there were a lot of extra expenses so I decided it was time to go back to work.

I got a job in a toy factory where they made Corgi cars. I was there for twenty years until I retired in 1980. Then I started minding my grand-children so that my daughter could go back to work and soon I found myself looking after my neighbours' kids as well. I didn't mind because I was on my own in the house. John had died in 1971. He was only fifty at the time.

I had wonderful times with my grandchildren. I'd take them to the park or to the pictures and sometimes we'd go out on the rowing lake at Singleton. I loved the rowing. It took me back to when I was a young girl on Scattery and my brother Jimmy would let me take the oars on the crossing over to Kilrush.'

Heart of the Matter
Bill O'Callaghan

Photographer Patrick McHugh

Dr. Bill O'Callaghan grew up in Lifford, Ennis, where his father commanded the 22nd Battalion, FCA. He studied medicine at University College Dublin and afterwards worked in several hospitals in the city before going to the USA to study cardiology. He now works as a cardiologist at the Mayo Clinic in Scottsdale, Arizona.

'I arrived at Duke University in North Carolina in 1983 and I spent three years training before being appointed to the faculty. At the time I had intended to return to Ireland but there were few openings for cardiologists there. Then in 1987 the world famous Mayo Clinic opened up in Arizona and I was offered a consultant position. I've been here ever since. I married my wife, Brenda Parker from Limerick, in 1980. Our son Conor was born in 1983 and daughters Emer and Orla in 1987 and 1989.

My work as a cardiologist means that I have specialised training in dealing with heart rhythm problems and blockages in heart arteries, so I suppose I can be described as both a heart electrician and a plumber! Modern technology has made a huge difference to my work. I can treat fast heart rhythms with invasive techniques to permanently eradicate the problem, or implant devices such as defibrillators to stop abnormal rhythms and prevent patients from dying suddenly from cardiac arrest. These procedures, among others, have revolutionised the treatment of heart disease and have made my work tremendously exciting and rewarding.

Arizona is quite a contrast to Co. Clare. We live in the desert which means sunny days all year round. However, the summers are very hot. It's difficult to ever imagine actually missing rain, but after months of desert sunshine, a "soft" Clare day would be nice. Though I live far away, I'm lucky to be able to return to Clare on holidays every year. The Internet, with the Irish papers and *The Clare Champion* on-line, keeps me in touch as the world becomes, daily, a much smaller place.'

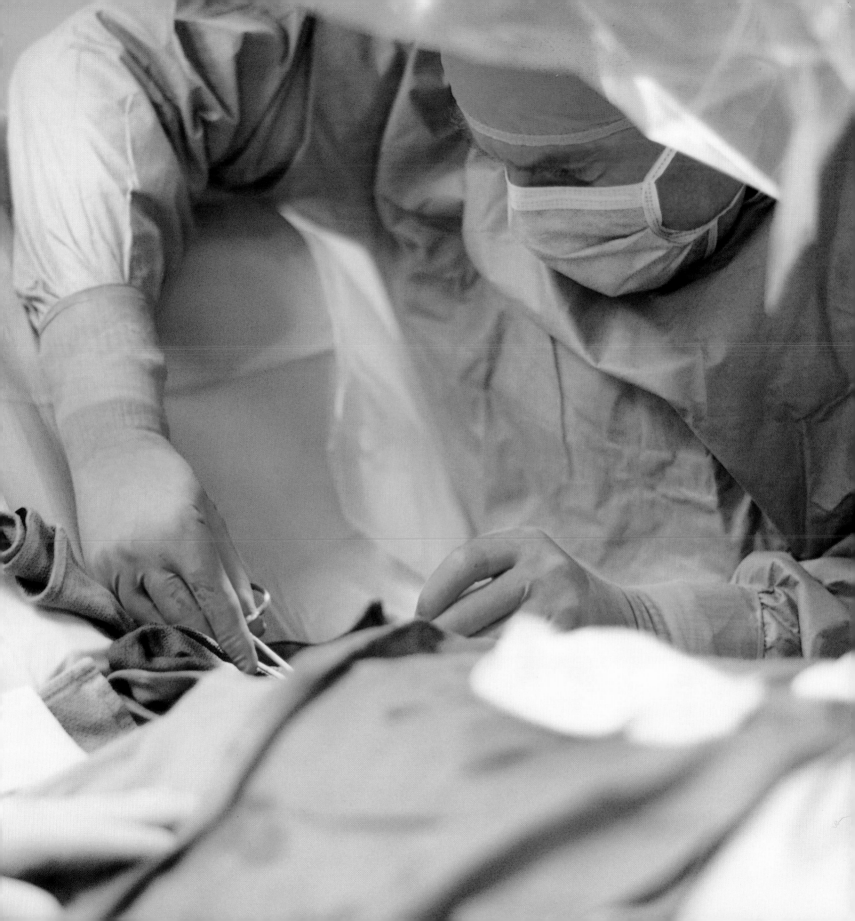

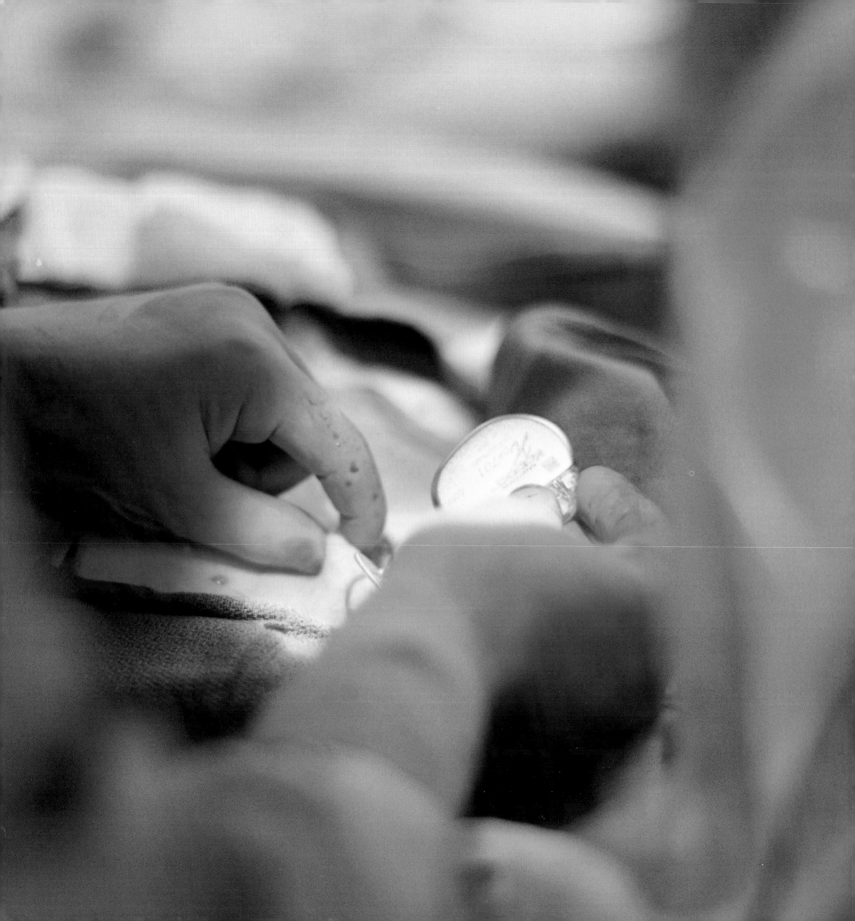

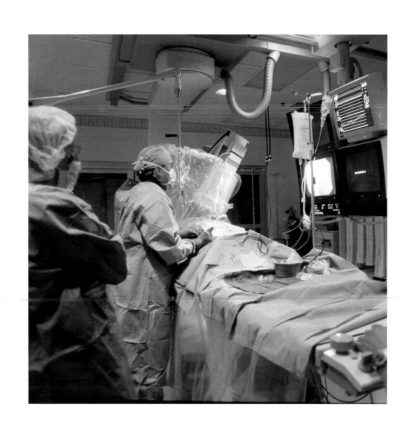

To the Lowlands of Holland
David Baker

Photographer Eamon Ward

Born in 1974, David Baker grew up in Newtown, Bodyke. After leaving school he trained as a carpenter before going to Holland.

'I worked around locally for a while after I left school and did a welding course with FÁS. Then Martin Lenihan from O'Callaghan's Mills took me on and I trained as a carpenter for four years. At that stage I wanted a change and I saw this ad in *The Clare Champion* looking for carpenters in Holland so I decided I'd give it a go. I didn't have anything to lose because there were free flights and accommodation included.

I ended up working in a factory making pre-cast shutters. The work here is different from back home. You start at six in the morning and finish at four in the afternoon. We work at weekends as well, and on Saturday mornings from five until ten. We're fairly well paid, so the hours aren't a big problem.

I'm here in The Hague with my girlfriend Claire O'Driscoll, so our evenings and weekends are fairly quiet. We don't go cracked on drugs or anything like some of the Irish lads out here. There's a pub nearby called the Spring Bar run by Liam Minogue from Clare and we go there for a few pints and a chat.

Claire has always wanted to go to Australia so when we've saved up a bit of money we'll probably go there and see what it's like. The great thing about the way things are at home at the moment is that we could go back in the morning and both of us could walk into a job, no bother. That gives you great freedom because if you do want to get out and work some place else or travel a bit you can be sure you'll have something to come back to.

Not like in the old days. When you left that time, you were gone for good.'

In Vogue
Assumpta Clohessy

Photographer Patrick McHugh

Assumpta Clohessy comes from Caherea, Lissycasey. After leaving school she trained as a hairdresser before going to New York in 1986. She then worked in several European capitals before returning to the United States.

'For as long as I can remember I've had a fascination with beauty. After I left school I did a four-year hairdressing apprenticeship in Ennis. When I qualified, I wanted to see some of the world so I headed for New York. I can still remember my first impressions of the place with all its colour and excitement and total madness. I loved it.

Like most of the Irish in New York in the 1980s I was an illegal immigrant and it was hard to get good work so I moved to London where I became assistant manager at a city centre salon. Soon though, I was back in New York taking night classes in the art of make-up. Then I began to work with fashion photographers doing hair and make-up for models. I realised that I really wanted to make a career of this but I knew I'd have to leave New York again to get the experience I needed. This time I headed for Spain.

After Madrid I moved to Dublin and got myself an agent. I began to work for fashion magazines, advertising agencies and catalogue and beauty companies. Around that time my Green Card came through and New York beckoned once again. After a four–year absence I returned, and I've been here since.

Now I have an agent here in New York who sends my portfolio out to potential clients. I work mainly in photo studios in Manhattan but frequently I'm out of New York, working all over the States. I do shoots for European and American fashion magazines, celebrity magazines, catalogues, CD covers and advertising campaigns. New York is a great place to live and work, probably the best place in the world for what I do. But a big part of me is still back home in Clare and, I think, always will be.'

Beneath the Southern Cross
Micheal Cleary

Photographer John Kelly

Michael Cleary was born in Darragh in 1916. After attending
agricultural college he worked in Mayo for several years with
the Department of Agriculture before being transferred back
to Clare. In 1956 he went to England with his family. Later
they emigrated to Australia where he worked with the
Irrigation Commission until his retirement.

'I remember during the 1930s driving cattle to the fair, then
driving them back home not sold. We did that again and again.
Sometimes you wouldn't even get an offer for them.

After I finished school at the Christian Brothers in Ennis I went
to agricultural college. My first permanent job was with the
Department of Agriculture and they sent me to Ballycastle in
Mayo. That's where I met my wife, Mina Browne, and we
settled back in Lisdoonvarna. We were thirteen years there and
had three boys and two girls. As they got older we decided to
move to England where they could get a better education.
We went over in 1956 and I got a job with the National
Agricultural Advisory Service. Then, by the mid-1960s, the kids
were coming up to university age and the papers were full of
ads and articles about free college places in Australia. So we
packed our bags again and headed off down under.

I got a job with the Irrigation Commission where I had to
investigate complaints about access to water. I spent most
of my time working out in the bush, sometimes for weeks,
camping out beneath the Southern Cross. When the kids
were grown and gone Mina would come with me. I enjoyed
that time better than any other period in my life.

Mina died in her sleep late last year. We always did everything
together, we were like two goats tethered. I suppose when
you've made two moves to two strange countries you get very
close because you have to rely on each other for everything.
Australia is a great country but the people here aren't the
same. What I miss most about home is the closeness of the
people, the friends and the neighbours. You don't get that here
so much.'

Horseman of Negros
Micheal Doohan

Photographer Mike Mulcaire

Fr Michael Doohan was born at The Hand in the parish of Mullagh in 1928. After ordination as a member of the Missionary Society of St.Columban he went to the Philippines in 1953.

'Most young boys and girls in my time didn't get a secondary education. Instead they emigrated to England or America. After national school I went as a day-boy to Flannan's, boarding in the town of Ennis and cycling home at the weekends to get the next week's provisions. My experiences in those years were good training for the missions later on.

My older brother, Fr John, had gone to the seminary at Dalgan Park and I'm sure that influenced my decision to follow the missionary life. I spent seven years studying at Dalgan Park and then I was sent to the Philippines. My brother was already there so that made leaving home and family a little easier. The journey by boat from San Francisco to Manila took twenty-one days. We had no language schools then so when I got there I had to learn to communicate by trial and error.

I settled in quickly enough, and my first parish assignment was in the mountains. It was remote and isolated with few roads. However, my West Clare upbringing proved to be my salvation. I grew up during the war when even bicycle tyres were scarce so I was well used to horse and saddle from an early age. That love for horses and ponies has served me well here as sometimes I have had to cover distances of twenty miles or more several times a week.

I still ride a horse, or sometimes a mountain pony, around my present parish. I find it's great for exercise and it helps to keep my reflexes sharp. You have to be alert, even with a quiet horse and I'm not forgetting I was born back in 1928. It's been a great life so far and I hope to keep it that way for a while yet.'

Maybe One Day
Carmel Burns

Photographer Patrick McHugh

Born in 1969, Carmel Burns comes from Glascloune, Doonbeg. After leaving school she went to Chicago where she spent some time as a waitress. She currently works as a nanny.

'On 14 October 1987 I left Shannon Airport, bound for Chicago. My decision to emigrate wasn't monumental in itself nor were the reasons behind it compelling. I was young, I had a desire to travel and the biggest hurdle for me at the time was to settle on a destination. I had originally chosen New York, but a friend of mine had family in Chicago so we travelled together to the Windy City.

My first job here was as a waitress in a Greek restaurant. This was quite a challenge. The city was very new and strange to me and for the first time in my life I was totally responsible for supporting myself. I stayed in that job for a few years and then I met the Peards. They were a young family looking for a nanny on a temporary basis. I was interested in the job, so they took me on. I'm still with them today and I also nanny part time for another family, the Ryans. Being a nanny is like being part of the family. I have been very fortunate with the two families I've worked for. Not only do we get on really well but I've travelled with them extensively in the US and the Caribbean. It's one of the great perks of the job.

I go home every Christmas to Glascloune. It's great to see all my family and friends again. I love sitting on "the long couch", watching *Coronation Street* and drinking Bulmers. All the comforts of home! I only wish that Chicago and Glascloune weren't as far apart as they are.

When I emigrated in 1987 I didn't leave with the intention of being away this long. There are days here in Chicago when I think to myself "I'm going to move back home". Who knows, maybe one day I will.'

A Touch of Glass
Patrick Manning

Photographer Christy McNamara

Patrick Manning was born and grew up in Ennis. After studying Agriculture at University College Dublin he worked with Dublin Corporation for several years before embarking on a career as an architect. In 1993 he moved to Lima where he now owns and manages the largest stained glass studio in Peru.

'Back in 1981 while travelling in China I was invited to a meal and discovered to my horror that the main course was roast dog. Initially I felt nauseated but then I realised that it was my own Western conditioning that made me feel that way. I understood for the first time that life is constantly changing and that we must be open to and accept such changes. By adopting this approach we can enjoy life all the more, no matter where we are living. Needless to say I finished the meal with a whole new perspective on life.

In 1986 I left Ireland for London where I worked and studied until 1992. It was while I was there that I met Rocio, my Peruvian-born wife. In 1989 we were married and in 1993 decided to move to Peru. Once in Lima I set up a stained glass studio, called Glasstek. Today Glasstek is the largest stained glass studio in Peru, handling residential, religious and commercial commissions.

Here in Peru the warmth of the people and the scenery are very similar to that of Ireland. Sometimes I miss Clare, but thanks to e-mail and more airline services, I am constantly in touch with friends and family. Apart from the people and the music, what I really miss are the simple things such as home–made bread and tea! But there is so much to do here in Peru–the Amazon jungle to visit, the Andes for trekking and climbing, lost cities to explore and finally the beaches for relaxing. Sometimes you feel that there are not enough hours in the day as anyone who has visited Peru will tell you!'

No Ordinary Life
Maura Kavanagh

Photographer Veronica Nicholson

Maura Kavanagh (née Collins) grew up in Ennis in the 1950s. She trained as a primary school teacher and has worked in Dublin and Kildare. In 1997 her husband Michael, an Irish Army Officer was posted to the UN in Cyprus and Maura took leave of absence from her job to go with him.

'I grew up just opposite the Fair Green gate in Ennis and I can still remember all the animals arriving for that day's fair. Anyone from Ennis can easily judge my vintage from that one.My first job was teaching inner city kids in Gardiner Street in Dublin. Around that time I met my husband Mick Kavanagh, who was in the army and after we married we moved to Newbridge in Co. Kildare where I got a job teaching in Naas. We have three children, two daughters and one son.

When my husband got a tour of duty with the UN in Cyprus I decided to take a chance and go with him. I had no experience of living abroad and it was going to be a big change from what had been a very ordinary life for me back home.

Although Cyprus is very Mediterranean and exotic in many ways, it's a lot like the way Ireland was back in the late 1950s. The older people are very religious and the old women in their black shawls remind me of the women I used to see praying in the Friary in Ennis. Life here is very much centred around the family and each family takes responsibility for all its members.

The local Greek Cypriots here are very much aware of Ireland and because they live on a disputed island themselves, they have a keen interest in the progress of our own peace process.

Meeting all the different people from around the world who work here in the UN has been amazing, Australians, Canadians, Hungarians, Finns, Argentinians—I don't know how I'll be able to settle down to ordinary everyday life when I get back home.'

In the Holy City
Eugene Nugent

Photographer Veronica Nicholson

Monsignor Eugene Nugent grew up in Gortaderra near Scariff. After studying for the priesthood in Maynooth and Rome he was ordained in 1983. Later he returned to study in Rome and in 1990 he was appointed to the Vatican Diplomatic Service. He is currently First Secretary to the Apostolic Nunciature in Israel and is based in Jerusalem.

'I was born on 21 October 1958, a few days after the death of Pope Pius XII, also known as Eugene Pacelli. It was my godmother Bridget Minogue who suggested the name Eugene for me, after the Pope. For as long as I can remember, I always wanted to be a priest and after I did my Leaving at the secondary school in Scariff I started my studies in Maynooth. After graduating in 1979, I went to study theology in Rome. I was ordained in Scariff in July 1983, and the following year I was appointed a curate in Ennis. I worked there until 1987 when I returned to Rome, this time to do a doctorate in Canon Law.

One day I got a call from Bishop Harty saying that he had been asked to release me to work in the Secretariat of State at the Vatican and I spent the next three years there at the English language section.

In 1990 I was asked to enter the Holy See's diplomatic service and attended the Pontifical Academy for two years. I was then appointed Attaché at the Nunciature in Ankara and in July 1996 I was transferred to my present location, Jerusalem.

Since coming here my work has been interesting and varied. As a member of the Bilateral Working Commission, I have been involved in negotiating two treaties, one between Israel and the Holy See and the other between the Holy See and the Palestinian Authority. The preparations for the Pope's historic visit to the Holy Land kept me busy for most of the past year.

I've been here for almost four years now so I expect another transfer soon. Where to, only God knows!'

Dancing on the Tables
Kevin Morrissey

Photographer Mike Mulcaire

Born in 1974, Kevin Morrissey grew up in Clarecastle. While studying in Galway he began working in the bar trade and in 1998 accepted an offer to manage The Irish Pub in Frankfurt.

'When I finished college I found myself managing Monroe's Bar in Galway and it was there I heard about the job in Germany. I didn't speak any German but I thought it was worth a try. A few weeks later I was over here in Frankfurt managing the oldest Irish pub on the continent.

The Irish Pub was opened twenty-eight years ago by a Dublin man who saw a gap in the market. He was a bit before his time because it's only in the last ten years or so that the Irish theme pub has really taken off around Europe. A lot of the newer ones don't have any Irish involvement or management. Here it's different. For a start, all the staff must be able to speak English and be Irish if possible. Most of our customers here aren't German at all. Frankfurt is a very international city so along with the Irish we get a lot of Americans, British and Australians.

The bar trade here is different to Ireland. In Germany you're always thinking up something new to offer your customers like party nights and different promotions. The best nights though are when there's a good crowd of Irish in. Lads who'd sit quietly sipping a pint in the corner of their local back home can end up dancing on the tables out here with very little on. I don't know, it's just something that seems to come over the Irish abroad. I've even been known to pick up a guitar and sing. But that's mostly just to clear the place at closing time. One verse of "American Pie" usually does it.

I'd like to have my own place some day, maybe here in Germany or back in Clare. In the meantime, I'm enjoying the craic, seeing a bit of the world and learning some German into the bargain.'

Making a Difference
Eamonn Meehan

Photographer Eamon Ward

Eamonn Meehan was born in Kilmaley in 1956. After training as a primary school teacher, he taught in Kildare before going to work in Kenya for two years. He went back to Africa in 1987 and on his return to Ireland joined Trócaire where he has worked ever since.

'It was while I was teaching in Clane, Co. Kildare that I realised I wanted to try something different. I didn't want to do the usual thing like heading off to the USA or Australia so I decided to go to Kenya for a couple of years. I worked as a teacher there and it opened my eyes to some of the realities of life in our world, especially how those in developing countries live. I felt that here was an area where I could make a difference.

I went back to Africa again in 1987 and worked in Lesotho for APSO, the Agency for Personal Service Overseas. When I returned to Ireland, I joined Trócaire where I feel I have found a true spiritual and professional home.

In a world where millions of children die each year from readily preventable diseases and where tens of millions don't have enough to eat, Trócaire's belief in tackling the root causes of injustice and underdevelopment still has a powerful influence on me. While working with Trócaire I have travelled widely in the developing world but mostly in Africa. I am always amazed and inspired by the dignity and courage of the people I meet and I have no doubt that eventually, the struggle to end absolute poverty will be successful.

I try to get back to Clare every few months to visit my parents in Kilmaley and the rest of my family. Despite my many trips overseas, I always find a strong pull home. I always look forward to catching up on the news and having a few pints while listening to the music in Ciaran's Bar on a Saturday night. Then I know that Clare is the place where I really belong.'

A Night at the Opera
Marie Hegarty

Photographer Eamon Ward

Catherine (Marie) Hegarty grew up in Ennistymon. She studied singing with Dr Veronica Dunne in Dublin before going to opera school in London. She has now embarked on a career as a professional opera singer.

'I was just seven when I gave my first public performance. It was on the back of a truck at a Feis Cheoil in Kilrush and I came home with two gold medals in my pocket. Later on at the Convent of Mercy Secondary School in Ennistymon I was involved with the choirs and *sean nós* singing.

After leaving school I worked at everything from cleaning to hotel reception. Then, following an audition, the great singer and teacher Veronica Dunne took me on as a student. Three years later I was being offered scholarships to all the major opera schools in England. The Aillwee Caves offered to sponsor my studies and have been a great help to me ever since.

Early on I began to realise the commitment and hard work involved in becoming a professional singer. It's not uncommon to work ten or twelve hour-days, seven days a week.

I did my postgraduate study at the Guildhall School of Music and Drama in London and while there I sang seven opera roles and performed in the Far East, Middle East and the USA. Nominated by the Guildhall to audition for the National Opera Studio, I won one of ten coveted places to study under some of Europe's greatest coaches. The schedule was gruelling involving hours of classes and then public performances with the Welsh National Opera Orchestra, the English National Opera and appearances at the Royal Opera House Covent Garden and the Queen Elizabeth Hall in London.

What I love about what I'm doing is that there's always something new to learn. Not a day goes by that I don't realise how lucky I am to have this unique talent and the wonderful support of family and friends that have made it all possible.'

Stone Mad
Seán Noonan

Photographer Christy McNamara

Seán Noonan grew up in Ennis in the 1950s. He lived for a time in Broadford and after working at several jobs he discovered his talent for building stone walls. He emigrated to the USA in the mid-1980s. He now lives in Connecticut with his wife and daughter.

'After leaving school I had a few jobs but couldn't settle at any of them. Then I got a job that involved repairing walls for some farmers and found I had a knack for it. I had no conscious intention of making the laying up of stone a core segment of my life. It just seemed to happen. Around that time, I met my future wife, an American girl who was over here on holidays. After three years of transatlantic letters and several journeys, we married in 1978 and lived for a while near Corofin. By the mid-1980s, however, the Irish economy was doing badly so, after our daughter was born, we decided to go to the States.

When I arrived here I thought I would never have to lift a stone again but that lasted only a short while. The demand for stone wall construction, chimney work, and patio laying was limitless and so I became my own boss again. We bought a piece of land and I built a timber frame house, doing all the work myself. That truly anchored me to this area and now that I have made a name for myself in my trade I would find it hard to start over somewhere else.

For me, the most painful aspect of settling in the States was the level of anonymity. People are far more private here, compared to Ireland and are far less easygoing and sociable. That's what I miss most.

I still reflect on the good old days in Ireland and on the people who made a mark on my life. When you leave a place at a particular time, the image you take with you of that place and its people becomes frozen in time, like a fly in amber.'

On Four Continents
Frank Sweeney

Photographer Mike Mulcaire

Born in 1960, Frank Sweeney grew up on Kevin Barry Avenue in Ennis. He studied engineering at University College Dublin before embarking on a career that has seen him work on four continents. He is currently involved in the construction of a power station in North-East China.

'My early years were fairly typical of most young Irish people growing up in the 1960s and 1970s—Gaelic games, Holy Communion, Confirmation, the Bothy Band, and the Christian Brothers!

When I left Ireland in the mid-1980s, I fulfilled a childhood dream, working for three years in Africa. Zimbabwe made a lasting impression on me and I took a piece of it with me when I left. I met my wife Connie there and we were married in 1986.

I tried to get closer to home then, living in England for six years but the travel bug hit again and I dragged my wife and family to Athens where we stayed for five years. In 1996 I was sent to Chicago for nine months. It was hard to leave my pregnant wife back in Athens with no relatives around to support her. I was glad to get my young family back together in June 1997 when we settled in Orlando, Florida. Our fourth child was born in August that year.

Now I'm away again, this time in China. A consortium of British and American companies have supplied four coal-fired power plants to the Chinese and I'm involved in the design and procurement of the equipment. The people here are warm, friendly, curious and courteous. You are treated like an honoured guest. However, the Chinese are shrewd businessmen and tough negotiators. I've learned a lot from them.

I'm away from Clare nineteen years now and like many before me, I never intended to stay away that long. But, like every other Irishman, when I do get home I find myself talking for hours and hours about where I've been and what's changed since I've been gone. When I think about home, its probably the great conversations that I miss the most.'

The Road to Gaborone
Michael Connolly

Photographer Eamon Ward

Michael Connolly comes from Ennis. After qualifying as an architect in 1981 he worked in Ireland throughout the 1980s before the economic recession forced him to seek work abroad. He got a job in Gaborone, Botswana where he still lives and works.

'I remember going for the interview for the job in Botswana. It was in Dublin on St. Patrick's Day, 1988, and it was cold and wet–very wet! Then, six weeks later we were in Gaborone under a blazing sun and a cloudless sky. My wife Ita and myself decided we'd stay for two years, maximum. Then in 1990 I joined the firm of Anderson and Anderson International in Gaborone and in 1997 became its Managing Director. Our major contributions to the city skyline to date include the Headquarters for the Central Bank of Botswana and the Botswana Technology Centre.

It's now over twelve years since that first flight to Africa. We've moved house eight times and had three additions to the family. Siomha, born in 1991, Fergal in 1993, and Oisín in 1997. The children don't have Irish or even Clare accents but they are very aware of their heritage and are proud to be Irish in a city of so many different nationalities.

[127]

As well as being married to Ita I also feel that I'm married to the St. Patrick's Society, the central focus for the Irish population here in Gaborone. Ita has been actively involved in the society since we arrived and we are claiming the dubious distinction of having introduced the pub quiz to Botswana.

Naturally the party of the year is the St. Patrick's Night Gala Dinner. It has special significance for us. Not only do we acknowledge our national saint but also celebrate the anniversary of that job interview in a wet and windy Dublin all those years ago that set us on the road to Gaborone.'

In the News
Anne Flaherty

Photographer Veronica Nicholson

Born in 1959, Anne Flaherty grew up on the Gort Road in Ennis. She studied journalism in Dublin before embarking on a successful freelance career. She has reported for the BBC and RTE from around the world. She now lives in London with her husband, award-winning journalist Fergal Keane and their son Daniel.

'My first job as a journalist was with *The Clare News*. That lasted six months and then the paper closed down. After that *The Limerick Echo* took me on and while there I was offered a job at the *Irish Press* in Dublin. Both these papers have since closed—but only after I left them!

In the late 1980s I worked in Belfast covering the conflict there. I lived in the North for two years and freelanced for *The Irish Times*. Then in 1991, along with my husband Fergal, I moved to South Africa and covered the transition to democracy. While there I freelanced for most of the Irish media outlets, including RTE. They were exciting and dangerous years but we loved the variety and vastness of the country and missed it when we left for Hong Kong in 1994. There was lots of journalistic work to do there as Hong Kong approached the 1997 deadline for the handover to Chinese rule. While there I travelled all over Asia and learned to write Chinese calligraphy and speak some Cantonese. Hong Kong is very special to me because it was there our son Daniel was born in 1996.

We're back in London now where I continue to work as a freelance journalist which includes some radio work for the BBC. I miss the friendliness and the way of life at home so when I'm back I love driving around West Clare, the Burren and the wild Atlantic coast. Whenever I hear "Song for Ireland" I think of Clare and I feel nostalgic for home. But now at least I know it's only an hour away.'

Against the Tide
John Glynn

Photographer John Kelly

John Glynn was born in Kilkee in 1936. He left for Australia in the early 1960s and worked in Sydney before going to Papua New Guinea to become a teacher. In 1981 he was ordained a priest for the Diocese of Kavieng where he served until 1997 when his Bishop curtailed his ministry. He now lives in retirement on the island of New Ireland.

'I emigrated to Australia in 1961 and worked at several jobs in Sydney. They were happy years but I didn't feel settled in myself so in 1963 I headed for Papua New Guinea and trained as a teacher. Life there was hard but the people accepted me immediately with open hearts. I felt a sense of belonging, value and fulfillment that I had never had before. For several years I had been struggling with a sense of vocation and in 1975 I went to Australia to begin my studies for the priesthood. I returned to Papua New Guinea in 1981.

My ministry found me in remote island parishes, facing the danger of stormy seas, hunger when food was short and recurrent bouts of fever. But I loved my life and the work I was doing. Most of all, I loved the people I was living among. I became deeply involved with the Barok people helping them in their struggle with an exploitative logging company.

However, the Diocese in which I worked was run by an American missionary order and my presence there troubled them. They believed I had no business there. This was especially painful for me as I had become a citizen of Papua New Guinea and felt I was among my own people. In 1997 I received a letter from my Bishop requesting me not to return to my parish. However, I returned to New Ireland to live in retirement on a coconut plantation, supported by friends but forbidden by my Bishop to say Mass or exercise any of my priestly faculties in public without his approval. It seems a sad way to conclude a lifetime of service as a teacher and a priest in the country and amongst the people I have come to love so much. But in God's hands be it.'

Doonbeg to Dallas
Senan Fitzmartin

Photographer Christy McNamara

Senan Fitzmartin was born in Doonbeg in 1937. He emigrated to London in 1953 and later went to New York where he began working in construction. In 1976 he moved to Dallas, Texas where he set up his own construction company.

'When I was a young lad growing up in Doonbeg, I used to see the flying boats from Foynes passing overhead and I'd say to myself, "One day I'll be on that, one day I'll go to America".

I was sixteen when I caught the boat for England. The last thing my mother did was to give me a shoe polish brush. I still use it today and every time I take it out I say a prayer for her. I think she knew that if I polished my shoes every day, like she taught me, she'd never be forgotten.

I didn't like London much and all the time dreamed of going to America. Then on 16 March 1958 I got on a plane at Shannon bound for New York. I was only there six weeks when I arrived home one day to find a telegram on the table telling me my father had died. I didn't have the money to go home for the funeral. Instead I observed the old rules of mourning and I didn't go out to a dance or listen to music for the next twelve months.

I got a job in construction and as the years went by I worked my way up to superintendent. In 1962 I married Tina Judge from Crossmolina in Mayo and we had three kids—Michelle, Donald and Glenn. Now we have four grandchildren as well.

In 1976 I moved to Dallas, Texas and the following year I quit my job and went into business with a partner. We called ourselves Constructors and Associates and in the first year we did $4 million worth of business. Later I went out on my own and last year the company turned over $300 million. Now we have offices in Dallas, Houston, Austin, San Antonio, Fort Worth and Denver.

Some days Dallas and Doonbeg can seem a million miles apart. Then I hear a church bell and I think of Stephen Dillon taking us back to the bog after first Mass, or sitting around the only radio in the village down at Enright's listening to Michéal Ó hEithir. I wouldn't swap those memories for all the oil in Texas and believe me, there's a lot of it here!'

A Bed for the Night
Phil Edmonds

Photographer Christy McNamara

Phil Edmonds was born in 1951 in Killaloe. When he was fourteen his family emigrated to the USA where he finished his education. In the 1970s he became involved in movements for social justice and now runs a shelter for the homeless in Providence, Rhode Island.

'My mother, brothers Dick and Eamonn, sister Marian and myself all left Cobh on an ocean liner and arrived in a sweltering New York City, still in our heavy Irish clothes. I was astonished by the noise, the pace and the hugeness of it all.

After finishing high school I was given a scholarship to Providence College but because of my stuttering I soon realised that teaching was not an option for me. I also realised that I was not interested in a career that would result in attaining material wealth. So I left college, worked in several factories and hung around an inner city corner for some wild years! In the late 1970s I became immersed in the struggle for social justice and also got very involved with the US peace movement. Around this time I took up the tin whistle again, having learned to play it in Killaloe when I was a child. Along with four of my friends we formed a Celtic music band called Pendragon.

In 1984 I began to live and work at Amos House in exchange for room and board. Over the years Amos House has provided shelter and meals to hundreds of people daily and we have also campaigned on issues of social equality and justice. Some years ago I met a Cambodian Buddhist monk called Samdech Preah Maha and have now co-edited a book of his life and teachings. He has helped me to realise the importance of being at peace, no matter what life brings.

For the past few years I've been taking care of my ageing mother most evenings. What the future holds for me, I have no idea. However, I am interested in helping to form a very simple self sustainable rural community within bicycle distance of Providence.'

The Forgotten People
Noel O'Neill

Photographer Mike Mulcaire

Fr. Noel O'Neill comes from Francis Street in Ennis. After finishing secondary school he went on to study for the priesthood. He was ordained as a priest of the Missionary Society of St. Columban in 1956 and the following year went to Korea.

'I started in Dalgan Park in Navan in 1949 and seven years later was ordained. The following year, 1957, I left for South Korea. Throughout the 1960s and 1970s I worked in several parishes tending to the pastoral needs of the people and organising programmes to help alleviate poverty in the deprived areas of the city.

One day I was called to a hospital to administer the last rites to a mentally disabled girl. Just before she died she turned to me and said "Thank you". I realised that mine was probably the first act of kindness she had experienced in years, maybe in her whole life. From that day on I decided that my mission was to work with the mentally disabled.

Over the years since then I have championed the cause of the mentally disabled in South Korea. I called them the "Forgotten People" because they would be hidden away in a back room, seen as a source of shame for the family or abandoned in an institution out in the country. Gradually though, things have changed and long years of campaigning are paying off. Three years ago, for the first time, the government passed legislation funding group homes and now also provides support for vocational training centres.

The place where I work is called the Emmaus Centre after the story of Christ who met the disciples on the road to Emmaus. They didn't recognise him for who he was. It's the same with us. We need to see the Christ incarnate in the sick and the wounded. For me, they are the real prophets.'

Life's Great Adventure
Dominick Kelly

Photographer John Kelly

Major Dominick Kelly was born in Clonina, Cree in April 1915. At the age of nine he was taken to Paris to live with his aunt. He later moved to London and during the Second World War he operated under cover in occupied France. Now retired, he lives in a suburb of Brussels where he settled after the war.

'My aunt was governess to the family of the Duc de Massa who lived on the Avenue des Champs Elysées. It was hard to imagine a scene further from Clonina, Cree, all silverware and servants with the best of everything! I thought I'd landed on the moon at first but I quickly settled in, and soon was speaking perfect French.

After I finished school, I trained to be a teacher, but then I decided it wasn't for me and went to London where I joined the Metropolitan Police. It was while I was on the beat that I met my future wife, Zizi. When the war broke out I joined the army and, because of my language skills, I was transferred to the Special Operations Executive. In 1943 I was parachuted into occupied France and, operating undercover, I set up an evacuation line from Brussels to Madrid. Later, I found myself in Belgium organising airdrops of guns and ammunition. After the war I worked as a Public Prosecutor for the Allied administration in Germany. I was demobilised in 1949 and settled in Brussels.

I worked for a Belgian investment bank for several years, then embarked on a career in business. I retired in 1981. My dear wife Zizi died some years ago and now I live alone. But I have wonderful neighbours and friends and my children and grandchildren come to see me when they can. Sometimes when I look at them I see again that barefoot little boy back in Clonina setting out for Paris and life's great adventure.'

Under African Skies
Rachel Abraham

Photographer Eamon Ward

Born in 1971, Rachel Abraham comes from Clarecastle. After completing her studies at the Limerick School of Art and Design she took up a post as a lecturer in a teacher training college in Chinhoyi, Zimbabwe, through APSO, the Agency for Personal Service Overseas.

'I was delighted when I got the job in Zimbabwe but nothing prepares you for the reality of leaving family, home and friends. I was longing for a change though, and I wanted to see a different perspective on life. Zimbabwe certainly gave me that.

The cultural differences have been the greatest challenge. At the start, my strong Irish accent meant my students couldn't understand me. When I addressed the class as "lads" my female students asked why they were being ignored! Zimbabweans watched in amusement as I lay out in the sun to get a tan and they were amazed that I would turn down eating a steak for something vegetarian. As time went on, things changed. Without realising it, life in Zimbabwe has become more real to me than life back home in Clare. I've developed a healthy lack of interest in the sun, learned to play the Mbira, a local instrument, and now use local expressions when I speak. But some things never leave you. For example, my longing for things Western just gets stronger . . . I'd think nothing of hitching 250 kilometres for a pizza and a movie.

Now I am preparing to return home after two years. I don't know how I will settle in this "new" Ireland. Ennis has changed a lot in the time I've been away, so I'm told. I'm not sure how I'll cope with the grey skies and the miserable weather. I look forward to the "craic" but I'm worried about being a stranger in my own country. Still, I'm ready to go home, so I'm willing to take the chance.

As we say here in Zimbabwe, "Fambai Zvakanacka" or "Go Well"!'

An Unquenchable Grief
Edna O'Brien

Photographer Patrick McHugh

Edna O'Brien was born in Drewsboro, Scariff. Her first book, *The Country Girls,* was published to wide critical acclaim in 1960 and to date she has written seventeen novels, seven collections of short stories, several plays and screenplays. The following extract is from *Mother Ireland*, published by Weidenfeld and Nicolson in 1976.

'Euston Station was a jungle, grim and impersonal, the very pigeons looked man-made, and when I saw the faces of the English I thought not of the long catalogue of blood-letting but of murder stories I had read in the Sunday papers and that swarthy visiting English woman from long ago who brought corn caps and a powder puff stitched into her hanky. But I had got away. That was my victory. The real quarrel with Ireland began to burgeon in me then: I had thought of how it had warped me, and those around me, and their parents before them, all stooped by a variety of fears—fear of church, fear of gombeenism, fear of phantoms, fear of ridicule, fear of hunger, fear of annihilation, and fear of their own deeply ingrained aggression that can only strike a blow at each other not having the innate authority to strike at those who are higher.

Pity arose too, pity for a land so often denuded, pity for a people reluctant to admit that there is anything wrong. That is why we leave. Because we beg to differ. Because we dread the psychological choke. But leaving is only conditional. The person you are is anathema to the person you would like to be.

But time changes everything including our attitude to place. There is no such thing as a perpetual hatred no more than there are unambiguous states of earthly love. Hour after hour I can think of Ireland, I can imagine without going far wrong what is happening in any one of the little towns by day or by night, can see the tillage and the walled garden, see the spilt porter foam along the counters, I can hear the arguments and the ballads, hear the elevation bell and the prayers for the dead.

I open a book, a school book maybe, or a book of superstition, or a book of place names, and I have only to see the names of Ballyhooley or Raheen to be plunged into that world from which I have derived such richness and an unquenchable grief.'

A Welcome in Brooklyn
Mai Fitzgerald

Photographer Christy McNamara

Mai Fitzgerald (nee Clancy) was born at Caherscooba near Newmarket-on-Fergus in 1909. When she was sixteen she left for Boston. After working in domestic service she married and settled in Brooklyn, New York. She now lives in a retirement home in the Bronx.

'It was hard leaving home because in those days all the travel was by boat and you never knew when you'd get home again. We were hit by a fierce storm on the way over and the boat had to put into New York instead of Boston. I felt very lost. But I remembered the last thing my father said to me, "Don't talk to strangers and if you have to talk to anyone, only talk to a man in uniform!" So I found a policeman and told him that I had to get to my Uncle Mike's in Springfield, Massachusetts. He brought me to Travellers Aid who took care of me and put me on a train to Springfield.

I got a job as a domestic. It was hard work. We worked all day, every day, even at the weekends and only had Wednesday afternoons off. After a while I moved to Flatbush in Brooklyn and that's where I met a Kerry man called Mike Fitzgerald. We got married and had seven boys but only three of them survived after birth.

We had a happy house though, and we always had someone from Clare or Kerry calling. Whenever the young people would come over to New York they'd call to us first and we'd try to help them find their feet.

I'm ninety-one now and you could say I'm retired. My boys have all done well for themselves, I'm glad to say. My one regret in life is that I never got to see my parents again. In fact I didn't get back to Clare again until I was sixty-two years old. When I think about that it makes me sad.'

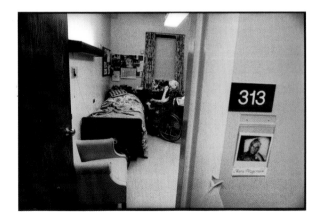

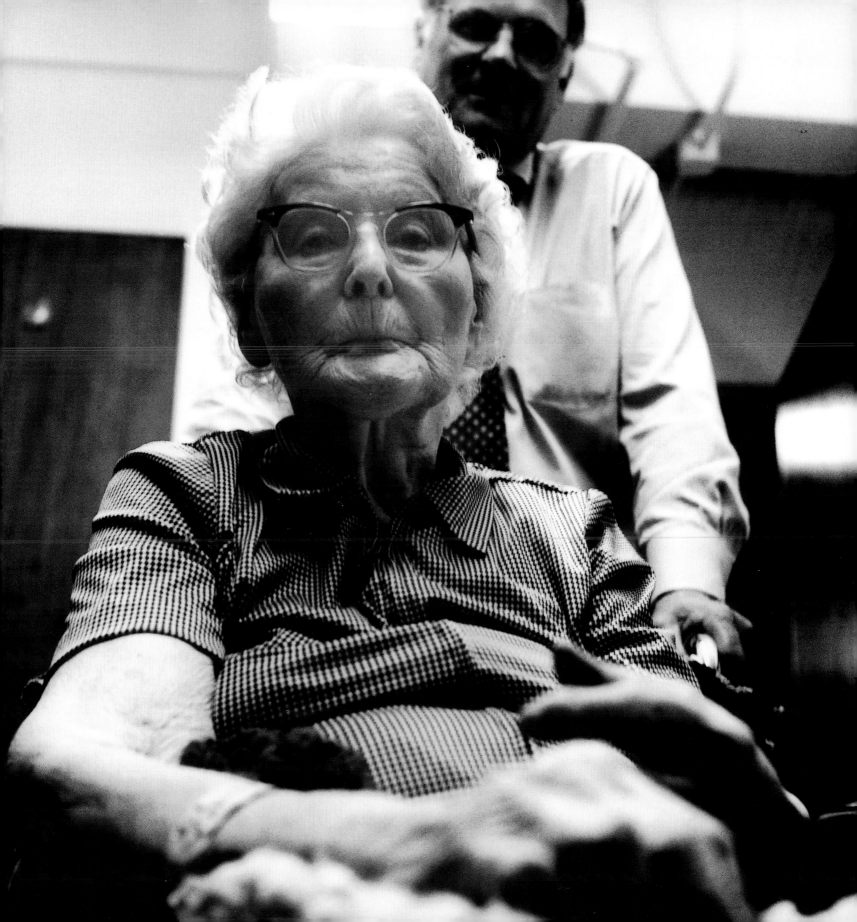

Between the Tracks
John Dilger

Photographer John Kelly

John Dilger was born in 1928 and grew up on the Kilrush Road in Ennis. At the age of twenty-two he went to England and later sailed for Australia. After working there for three years he moved to New Zealand where he married and settled in Auckland. Having worked all his life on the railways, he retired in 1989.

'In 1950 I went to England to an uncle of mine in Peterborough and worked on the railway. I wasn't very happy there so two years later I took the boat to Australia and ended up in Melbourne. I stayed three years there driving a tram.

I played a lot of sports in Melbourne—hurling, football and Australian rules. I even played cricket for the Tramway Club. I found my hurling grip very handy for the cricket and it's the same grip I still use to play golf today.

After a few years I got restless again and so I headed off to New Zealand and got a job as a train examiner in Auckland. That's where I met my wife Teresa and we married in 1957. She's from Hamilton but her father's and mother's parents came from Ireland. We have one son Patrick. He lives in the USA now.

I've always been a great sports fan all my life. The house here is full of thousands of match programmes that I've collected over the years. I'm still mad about hurling and I'm a great follower of the Clare team. I get all the games sent out to me on video and I have all the Clare hurling songs from the last few years.

Looking back now, I can't say I ever planned to end up on the other side of the world. But I do remember we had a neighbour at home, an old woman who used to read the tea-leaves. One day when I was a young lad she said to me "You're going to go over a lot of water". Well, I couldn't have gone any further, now could I?'

Sisters
Juliette O'Sullivan-Patel

Photographer Mike Mulcaire

Juliette O'Sullivan-Patel comes from Lissane, Clarecastle. After completing her education at Coláiste Muire she went on to train as a nurse. Later she joined her sister Catherine in London where she is now married.

'When I was growing up back in Ennis in the 1980s, emigration from Ireland was at an all-time high. We expected to have to leave to find work. So when I finished my training as a nurse I came over to London. My sister Catherine had moved here eight years before to work as a chef and she helped me to settle in.

I met Suresh while I was on a visit to Birmingham. For both of us it was love at first sight and we got married in Ennis in 1997. Now I'm expecting our first child.

In 1997 Catherine opened her own restaurant. It's called Arancia, which is the Italian for orange. Arancia has been a success from the beginning, winning Best New Restaurant in the Time Out awards for 1998. The menu is mainly rustic Italian and Mediterranean and has had rave reviews from *The Irish Times*, *The Evening Standard* and *Time Out*.

We get home to Clare about three times a year to see my mother and my sisters. We both miss our mother's cooking, especially the scones.

Many of my friends who came over around the same time as me are going back to Ireland now but I can't see myself doing that. To be honest, London is now my home.'

Famine Fighter
Mike McDonagh

Photographer Mike Mulcaire

Mike McDonagh was born in 1956 and grew up on Marian Avenue in Ennis. After working for several years with the Mid-Western Health Board, he joined Concern in 1983. Since then he has been based in seventeen countries, co-ordinating relief operations in disaster areas and war zones.

'When I started with Concern I was only going to stay a few years and then go back to my job with the Health Board. Instead, I decided to stay and I've been with Concern now for most of the past seventeen years.

Over the years I have worked in many countries. Inevitably some places stand out more than others—the extreme poverty in Bangladesh, which is only slightly bigger than Ireland but with a population of 125 million people, the famine in Somalia and the Irish aid workers' contribution to the relief effort, President Robinson's visit there, the appalling suffering in Angola especially from land mines and the smell of death all around Rwanda during the genocide. In North Korea I am just one of a hundred foreigners allowed to work in the country. Concern is one of six humanitarian organisations working there and the only Irish one.

Korea has been lucky for me. It is where I met my fiancée, Marzia Mongiorgi from Milan in Italy. I miss Clare especially when the Munster hurling championship comes around. Ireland is doing great now and the people are as generous as ever to organisations like Concern. If there is a black spot it is the less than warm welcome we give to refugees. However, it must be said that Ennis has a good record in this regard.

Working for Concern has given me tremendous satisfaction. We go where many other humanitarian organisations will not venture because of security concerns and are known for our professionalism and commonsense approach. Where I come from is also an advantage. Being Irish has helped me at many a road block in Africa.'

Real Madrid
Paul Casey

Photographer Eamon Ward

Paul Casey was born in 1969 and grew up in Ruan. After graduating from University College Cork, he left for Paris. A few years later his work took him to Madrid where he now lives with his partner and two-year-old daughter.

'When people here in Madrid ask me how many brothers and sisters I have I get a great kick out of naming the ten of them from Rosie to Brendan. I also tell them that if I was Spanish or French I wouldn't have been born because my turn would never have come around!

After school in Ruan and St Flannan's, I went to college in Cork and got a Diploma in Dairy Science. My father used to wonder how or why, since I could never even milk a cow at home. Despite this, Danone, the yogurt-makers in Paris, saw some potential in me and gave me a job. I'd wanted to go to France ever since I worked in my Auntie Berni's B&B one summer. That gave me my first contact with continentals and I wanted to see more.

I loved Paris and spent three great years there before the yogurt plant was shut down. But then Danone offered me the opportunity to work in Spain and now I'm at their International Yogurt and Fermented Milks Investigation Centre in Madrid.

This is a magical city and although the sea is far away, the blue sky more than makes up for it. The Spanish and the Irish are alike in many ways with family, sport, humour and religion playing a big part in our lives.

My girl friend Amila comes from Sarajevo and we have a beautiful daughter, Aila, who is two. We hope to get married next year. The Spanish say that the Irish are really Spanish people who got lost at sea. Well, I think there may be something in that because this exiled Clareman feels very much at home here.'

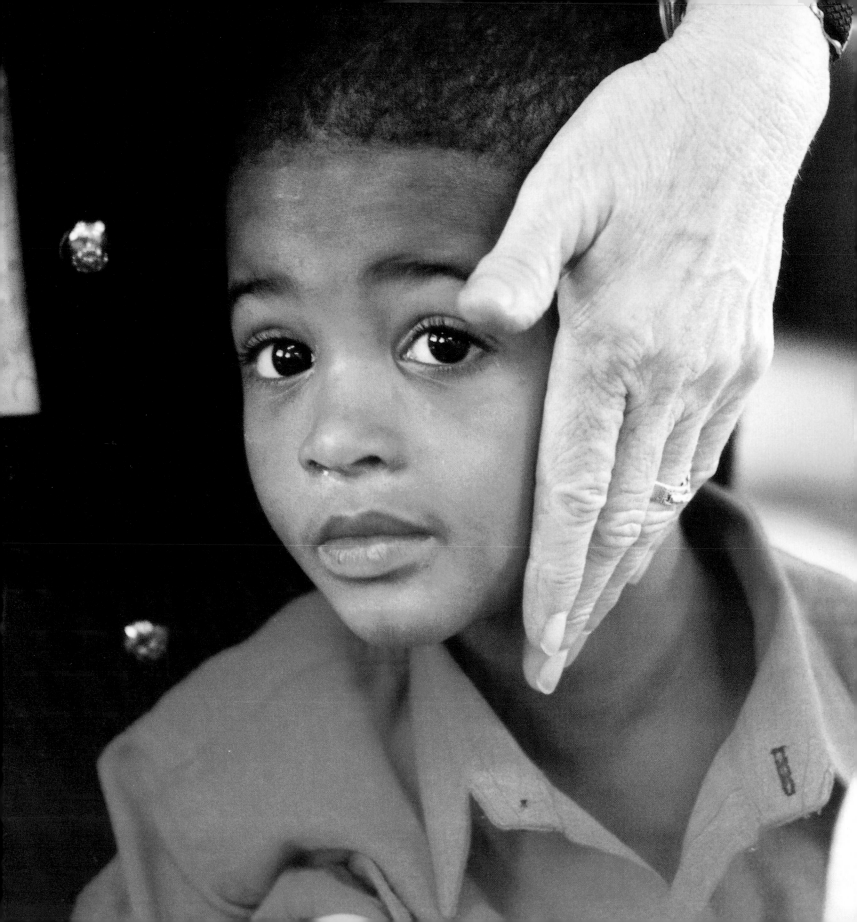

Despite the Odds
Ethel Normoyle

Photographer Eamon Ward

Sr. Ethel Normoyle was born in 1944 in Lissycasey. After leaving school she joined the Little Company of Mary Congregation. In 1972 she went to South Africa and now lives and works with the people of a shanty town outside Port Elizabeth.

'When I joined at first, everyone who knew me in Lissycasey thought I would last about a month. To be honest, I gave myself six weeks! After eight years with the Congregation in Ireland I was asked to work in South Africa. It was difficult, knowing I would have to leave behind those who meant everything to me—my parents and family, neighbours and friends. Now, twenty-eight years on and half a lifetime later there isn't a day that I don't miss Clare and yearn for home in Lissycasey.

My work in South Africa then, as now, was among the poor and marginalised. In 1988 I began work in Mission Vale, a sprawling shanty town of 50,000 people in the northern suburbs of Port Elizabeth. The people here are deprived of even the most basic necessities of life, lacking in shelter, nutrition, healthcare, and any form of employment. They are devastated by TB and HIV/AIDS. Addiction is rampant as is the physical and sexual abuse of women and children.

When I am tempted to despair I remember all the things we have achieved together, despite the odds. We have opened a medical centre, a pre-school, a nutrition unit, a community hall, a centre for street children, an information and human rights office and a counselling service.

And, even in the midst of the inevitable tears, we have fun. We laugh a lot together. I find a kinship with these people and my own people of West Clare. Both have endured centuries of struggle with a rugged and unyielding terrain. Yet both transcended that struggle through the haunting beauty of their traditional music. To the people of Clare and the people of Mission Vale I want to say that from living among you I have received far more than I could ever give.'

Real Life Story
Maura O'Connell

Photographer Christy McNamara

Maura O'Connell was born in Ennis in 1958 and grew up on Upper Market Street in the town. She performed with De Dannan in the early 1980s before embarking on a solo singing career. To date she has recorded six albums including *Just in Time*, *Blue is the Colour of Hope* and *Real Life Story* and has been nominated for a Grammy Award. She now lives in Nashville with her husband and son.

'My grandmother and my Aunt Bella both were great dancers, but it was from my mother, Amby, that I got my voice. She taught us all to sing a party piece as soon as we could speak and later we all sang in the Cathedral Choir and with the Ennis Musical Society. My father Frank was the actor in the family and I think it was this family background that gave me the confidence to pursue a career in music. When I was a teenager, Ennis was full of great musicians. Mike Hanrahan and I had a duo we called Tumbleweed. He later went on to great success with Stockton's Wing.

I came over to Nashville to make my first solo album and it's been my home now for fifteen years. My husband Mac and I got married in Ennis and our friends and his family still talk about what a great time they had. They'd never been to an Irish wedding before!

Tennessee is really beautiful and in the fall and winter I walk outside a lot. In the summertime though, I mostly stay indoors, away from the heat. Then I dream of a soft wind coming in from the west coast of Clare and gently cooling me down.

When I think about home, I think about the Ennis I knew as a child, a town balanced between two times, the old and the new. I was privileged to know people from that other time—a time without all our modern gadgets and no hint of any Celtic Tigers, a time of strong friendships and pride of place. It has served me well in all my travels. It is my touchstone, my inspiration and the "town I love so well".'

Digging for Gold
Declan Costelloe

Photographer Christy McNamara

Born in 1965, Declan Costelloe comes from Cappahard in Ennis. After graduating from University College Galway he studied mining geology at Cardiff University. His career as a geologist has taken him all over the world and he is currently based in Denver, Colorado.

'When I was still quite young I was fascinated by the fossils of plants and animals preserved in the Co. Clare limestone. At the time I never imagined I'd end up working in a business involving such a direct link to rocks.

Over the years I've worked with various companies, participating in and eventually managing projects on every continent. I've worked in exploration, where companies look for gold, and in mining where gold is produced from rocks in the ground. One of my favourite projects was based close to Kalgoorlie in West Australia. Today there is a statue of a prospector on the corner of Hannon Street in the town. It reminds locals and visitors that it was Paddy Hannon from Quin, a Clareman, who first found gold there in the 1870s.

My work has brought me to some of the remotest places on the planet where getting to work is never as simple as catching a bus. In French Guyana in South America, for example, I arrived at the site by aircraft and left in a dug-out canoe. But it isn't always travel. I've been lucky to have met and married a lovely lady from Wales called Ann-Marie. She has the patience to accept that my work often takes me to far-off lands and has also given me a good reason to come back and stay in one place for a reasonable amount of time!

Over the years I dreamed about setting up my own mining operation. Now I've formed a company aimed at developing gold deposits that other companies have rejected or abandoned. It's always a huge challenge to discover and develop a mine. But when you finally pour a bar of gold there's great satisfaction in knowing that all the time and effort has been worthwhile.'

A Matter of Faith
Alan Keane

Photographer Veronica Nicholson

Alan Keane was born in Ennis in 1952. Having travelled the world as a ship's radio officer he returned to Ireland where he qualified as an engineer and spent several years working in Dublin. He now lives and works at the world centre of the Bahá'í faith in Haifa, Israel.

'When I left school I trained as a radio officer in Limerick and spent a year at sea travelling to Europe, Africa and South America. Later I studied engineering at Kevin Street College of Technology in Dublin and then worked for an electrical engineering company there.

I first heard of the Bahá'í faith in the early 1970s and initially I wasn't very interested. But as I read more about it and attended meetings I discovered it was a very noble faith with many wonderful teachings that seemed to make sense for me and the world I was living in. Finally I decided that by becoming a Bahá'í I would not be abandoning my previous beliefs but rather would be taking them with me to the next stage of my own spiritual journey.

For the last sixteen years I have been living in Haifa which is the world centre for the Bahá'í faith and I have assisted in a major construction programme taking place here.

Being a member of the Bahá'í community gives me a strong sense of connection with all the peoples of the world. The Bahá'í faith is found in 235 countries with five million people worldwide. At the heart of our belief is the conviction that humanity is a single people with a common destiny. In the words of Bahá'u'lláh, the founder of our faith, "The earth is but one country and mankind its citizens".'

In the Shadow of the Black Christ
Moira Noonan

Photographer Christy McNamara

Sr. Moira Noonan was born in Caher in 1938. In 1952 she left Ireland and travelled to Houston, Texas as a postulant with the Sisters of Charity of the Incarnate Word. Over the years, her work with the Order has taken her all over North and Central America and she is now based in Guatemala where she runs a nursing home for the elderly and a detoxification facility for recovering alcoholics.

'I joined the novitiate of the Sisters of Charity of the Incarnate Word at Carrigoran near Newmarket-on-Fergus before leaving for the States in September 1952.

I was only fourteen at the time and my mother wrote the day and date of my leaving on the back of a miniature Sacred Heart picture which she put up on the wall at home. There it stayed undisturbed until the day I came back home for the first time as Sister Moira. That was in 1968, almost sixteen years later.

My work as a Sister of Charity took me right across the United States; from Texas to Utah, from Louisiana to California. Then in 1986 I was sent to Central America and ended up here in the town of Esquipulas in south-east Guatemala, a few kilometres from the border with Honduras and El Salvador. Esquipulas is a great centre of devotion with pilgrims and its great basilica dedicated to the Black Christ of Esquipulas is famous throughout Central America.

I am the administrator of "Hogar de mi Hermano" that means "Home of My Brother". It's a nursing home for the aged poor in and around Esquipulas, of which there are many. Recently I've set up a shelter for alcoholics to give them some place to live in a non-alcoholic environment while they are undergoing treatment.

I travel to the United States each year giving talks and raising funds for my nursing home and alcoholic centre. But I am always glad to get back to Esquipulas. Maybe it's because the green hills of Guatemala remind of the hills around Lough Graney back home.'

Best of the Bay
Maria Molony

Photographer Patrick McHugh

Born in 1965, Maria Molony grew up in Kincora Park in Ennis. She trained as a hair-stylist and spent some time in London before going to New York in 1986. She later moved to San Francisco where she now runs a successful hair and beauty business.

'After my twenty-first birthday party in Ennis, I headed off for New York. But I found it hard to get work with reputable hairdressing salons and so decided to waitress instead. Eventually the New York weather got the better of me so I left for San Francisco and am still here, twelve years later. After working in various salons in San Francisco a good friend, Brian Moloney also from Ennis, but no relation, advised me of a premises for rent and suggested that I open my own hair salon. With my parents' encouragement, "Máire Rua Hair Salon" opened on 1 December 1990.

It was tough going for a long time, but thank God, the hard work and long hours have now paid off and the business is thriving. So far we've received a "Best of the Bay" award and been voted one of the top 200 salons in the United States in 1999 and 2000. Last year, the opportunity presented itself to open another business and the "Maire Rua Body Salon" is now well and truly off the ground .

My eldest brother Brendan and younger sister Eileen have come out to San Francisco and are now settled into their own professions. My other brother Enda spent some time here as well, and is now living back in Ennis.

On Sundays I go to services at the Glide Memorial church. All denominations go there and the music is great. I volunteer what little time I have to the services that Glide provides for the homeless and less fortunate.

I love to go back to Ennis whenever I can to visit my family and friends. What the future holds, I don't know, but for the time being I'm happy to enjoy the life that San Francisco has to offer.'

[191]

A Soldier's Story
Pedro Scanlon

Photographer Eamon Ward

Patrick Scanlon was born on the Clare Road in Ennis in 1920. He emigrated to England when he was sixteen and worked as a labourer before joining the British Army. During the Second World War he fought in Africa and the Far East. He served again in Korea and was discharged in 1951. He then worked in the bar trade until he retired. Pedro Scanlon died in May 2000.

'When I signed up for the army I thought I'd do a few years, maybe see a bit of the world. I hadn't counted on the war coming so soon. I was stationed in Egypt first and then it was off to Palestine. Finally I ended up in India, on the border with Burma. Our job there was to keep the Japanese from breaking through.

After the war I found it hard to stick at any one job. I did a bit of work on the stalls in Portobello Market and one day I picked up a big Spanish hat, a sombrero. I used to wear it at the stall for a bit of a laugh and some of the regulars started to call me Pedro. It's stuck ever since.

In 1950 I was called up again to fight in Korea. The winter there was terrible. It was so cold you could only do sentry duty for thirty minutes at a time. I suffered severe frostbite and my hearing was badly damaged. I was discharged from the army on medical grounds in March 1951.

Again, I found it hard to settle at anything. I went back to the stall in Portobello for a while and did some casual work on the buildings and in pubs. Then I got a full time job at the Princess Alexandra in Kensington and I lived over the pub. I was there for about fifteen years until the place was sold up and I had to move. My nephew Michael helped me out then and I got the little flat I'm living in now. I'm very happy there. Would you believe this is the first time I've ever had the key to a front door of my own?'

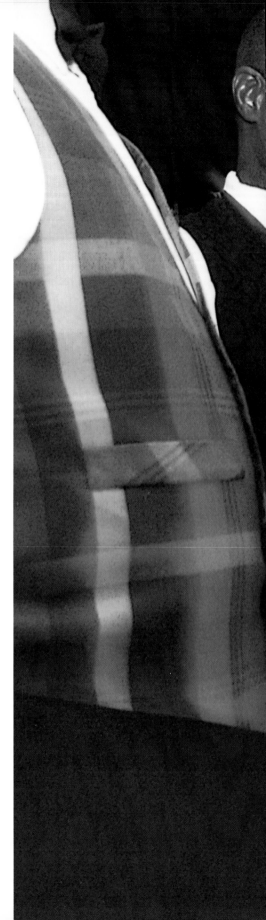

Bound for Bulawayo
Tess Simpson

Photographer Eamon Ward

Tess Simpson (nee Devaney) was born in the parish of Inch, four miles west of Ennis. She emigrated to Africa in 1946, settling in what was then Rhodesia.

'When we left for Africa my sister Mary and I had to travel to Holland first. There we caught a boat that was taking a thousand Dutch emigrants to settle in South Africa. We were travelling out to our aunt and uncle who lived in Rhodesia, now Zimbabwe.

The boat journey took sixteen days. Then, after arriving in Capetown, we had to travel four days by train up through Africa bound for Bulawayo. I remember being really surprised to find out how many Irish people were in the city, all part of a flourishing Irish association. I soon got involved and we met every Friday evening in a local hall. I met my future husband shortly afterwards. He worked for the country's newspaper group and so was transferred to various parts of the country. I got to see quite a lot of Rhodesia in this way. Eventually we returned to the capital Harare where my husband retired as managing director after serving forty-five years with the newspaper. We had three children, all of whom now live in Johannesburg. I'm happy to say that I am the proud grandmother of seven beautiful grandchildren!

I've enjoyed many trips back to Clare over the years. It isn't the long journey it used to be. I just get on a plane and I'm in Shannon in a few hours. In fact I arrived into Shannon Airport on that great day back in September 1995 when Clare won the All-Ireland Hurling Championship for the first time in eighty-one years. I'm here in Africa fifty-three years now. I've lived through some stirring times, with great upheavals and change as the country transformed from Rhodesia into Zimbabwe. That process of change is still going on.

All things considered though, it's been a wonderful experience, something I could never have dreamed off when I said goodbye to my family and friends in Inch over fifty years ago.'

On the Other Side of the World
Noel Whyte

Photographer John Kelly

Noel Whyte was born in 1959 and grew up in Kincora Park in Ennis. After finishing school he worked for a time with the Civil Service in Dublin. In 1986 he visited Australia for the first time. Two years later he returned there for good and now works in the corporate finance section of a major Australian bank.

'When I was working for the Revenue Commissioners in Dublin a group of us would go to the Greek Islands for our holidays every year. That's where I met my first Australian backpackers travelling around the world. I knew that was what I had to do.

In 1986 my brother Aidan and I planned our escape. Armed with two backpacks and a couple of airline tickets we set out for Australia. I spent six months travelling around and fell in love with the place. I also fell in love with an English nurse called Rosie and after seeing most of south-east Asia, we came back home. But I couldn't re-adjust to life here.

In 1988 I made two big decisions. One was to marry Rosie, the other was to return to Australia for a couple of years. Now, twelve years later, we're still here.

In the meantime I've completed a university degree and have a Masters in Financial Management. I am currently Associate Director in the corporate finance division of one of the large Australian banks. We have three children now, Aidan, Cian and Saskia.

At times I find it difficult living away from Clare. That's where my family and a lot of my friends are. And no matter how you look at it, I'm still living on the other side of the world. But being here has its compensations. Australia isn't heavily populated so we're surrounded by unspoiled beauty. The locals are great, very up-front and hard-working and they love to party. Also I've found that being Irish down under is a definite plus. And did I mention the weather at all?'

Reaching Out
Margaret Hogan

Photographer Eamon Ward

Sr. Nora Margaret Hogan was born near Killimer in 1946. After leaving school she joined the Medical Missionaries of Mary. Following several years of religious and professional training she went to Tanzania in 1975.

'I entered the Order at a unique time in the history of religious life. It was a time of great renewal and energy and this helped to convince me that I had made the right choice. Then followed years of training with the Order and time spent at university where I studied psychology.

I first came here to Tanzania nearly twenty-five years ago and I have learned quite a lot about myself and the world since then. I have certainly been challenged to appreciate worldviews and belief systems sometimes very different to my own. My work in Tanzania has been in the field of mental health. I have worked in the University Hospital in Dar es Salaam, in teaching and research, as well as clinical work. As a psychologist, I deal with people who are emotionally disturbed and psychologically wounded in many different ways. Coming from another continent, it has been especially challenging for me, reaching out to them from the other side of a cultural divide.

My life as a missionary has only been possible because I have always known the great love and support of my parents who each cared for me in their own special way. The loyalty of my four sisters and their families has also been invaluable. My Order, too, has been like a family to me and helped me to grow and develop both spiritually and professionally.

When I think of all the many wonderful people who have shared my life's journey so far, I feel truly grateful and blessed.'

A Bit of Paradise
Eddie Stack

Photographer Patrick McHugh

Eddie Stack grew up in Ennistymon. A graduate in engineering from University College Galway, he now lives in San Francisco where he is artistic director of the Irish Arts Foundation.

'The first time I heard of California was when Mickey Daneen sang about it in my father's pub in Ennistymon. I was only a boy but I could see the place as plain as day: lumps of gold as big as spuds scattered all over the land like fallen apples and men, women and children with big sacks picking them up to their hearts' content. The skies were as blue as the Blessed Virgin's mantle, there were babbling streams and a warm bright sun. Mickey Daneen was singing about paradise!

I probably would have hit the States sooner but the 1960s in Ireland were too good to leave and anyway they lasted well into the 1980s. By the time I got there I was a writer of sorts and could play a bit of music. San Francisco was good to me and in less than a week I got a freelance job with the local Irish paper. Soon radio work came my way and then I began to sell stories to magazines and city newspapers.

In those years most of the Irish people I knew in San Francisco were illegal. Our outlook and notions on life were very different from the settled Irish immigrants and I began publishing a quarterly magazine to cater for the 'New Irish' as we were known. *The Island* magazine lasted for more than three years and became the corner stone for the Irish Arts Foundation in San Francisco. A decade later, the IAF is internationally known as the producer of the San Francisco Celtic Music and Arts Festival and Finnegans Awake, a festival of Irish writers.

I'm in constant contact with Ireland and spend a few months every year in Clare. Maybe I'll return for good some time and write stories or sing songs about California like Mickey Daneen did for those still at home who long to taste a bit of paradise!'

Japanese Lessons
Fiona Malone

Photographer Mike Mulcaire

Fiona Malone was born in Ennis in 1973. After graduating from University College Galway she qualified as a teacher before leaving for Japan in 1997.

'I knew nothing about Japan before coming here. When I arrived I was given a quaint traditional Japanese apartment equipped with a not so quaint traditional toilet and bathroom. When bathing, I have to sit on a small wooden stool and wash myself before stepping into a steaming tub where I soak for anything up to thirty minutes. It's not like our quick shower at home! Bathing here takes time and patience but it is a wonderful experience, as well as the perfect end to a busy day. I then go to sleep on a futon (unfolded each night) to the sound of croaking frogs in the nearby paddyfields.

I teach at an academic senior high school which prepares students for entrance to third level institutions. In theory I work from eight until five although overtime is essentially mandatory and certainly expected. The students are the greatest source of my job satisfaction. Warm, diligent and very good-natured, they offer me a friendly respite from an otherwise serious working environment.

I've been here three years now and have slowly grown accustomed to many of the Japanese ways which I have to admit, at the start, I found quite odd. I now bow instinctively wherever I am—in the car, on my bike, even on the phone. I also say "hai" a lot and take my shoes off and put them back on again dozens of times a day. I regularly eat raw fish and meat.

Being here has given me the opportunity to travel throughout the region and I've been to China, Indonesia, Malaysia and Thailand. My exploration of different cultures has made me look again at my own from a distance, with a new perspective. Just by being here, I've learned a lot about my own home, my family and my country. Mostly though, I've learned a lot about myself.'

A Place in the Sun
Patricia Frawley

Photographer Veronica Nicholson

Patricia Frawley was born in 1971 and grew up in Curraghmore, Killaloe. After graduating from the Shannon College of Hotel Management and University College Galway she worked for some time in England. In 1997 she moved to the United Arab Emirates where she still lives and works.

'I was working for the Jury's Hotel Group in Bristol when I heard that the Hilton in Dubai were looking for a sales manager. I hardly knew where Dubai was at the time but I knew I wanted to travel, so I applied. A few months later I found myself out here.

At the start it was a bit of a culture shock. This is a Muslim country and I found it strange seeing all the women in the streets dressed head to foot in black. But the United Arab Emirates is one of the more liberal of the Arab states and certainly in Dubai the atmosphere is similar to big western cities. Women can drive cars here, which isn't allowed in some other Muslim countries.

The lifestyle here is very good. Firstly, there is sunshine all year round, and coming from rainy East Clare that makes a big difference. It's great to come home in the evening and sit out in the sun! Then there are great recreation facilities such as golf and tennis and you're never too far away from the sea.

With the job I have now I get a house, a car and I don't pay any tax, so what I earn I get to keep. I know a lot of people here who came for a few years and then just stayed on. When I came out here first I said I'd stay for a minimum of two years and a maximum of five. I want to have enough saved to give me a head start when I get home. According to my plan, I've got another two years to go. We'll see what happens then.'

Keeping the Peace
Senan Downes

Photographer Veronica Nicholson

Lt. Col. Senan Downes comes from Derryard in the parish of Doonbeg. After leaving school he joined the Army Cadets and was commissioned in 1966. A former intercounty footballer, his career has seen him serve all over Ireland and on three tours of duty to the Lebanon.

'Overseas service plays an important part in the current role of the Defence Forces and I've been on several United Nations missions over the years including Cyprus in 1972, and the Sinai Desert in 1973. I also served as a military observer in Beirut, Cairo and the Golan Heights between 1984 and 1986 and spent some time in Iraq in 1988.

This is my third tour of duty in the Lebanon and our mission here is to implement UN Resolution 425 which is to verify the withdrawal of Israeli forces and restore Lebanese Government authority. Our area of operation includes fourteen villages with a total population of between 40,000 and 50,000 people. The religious breakdown of the villages is 95 per cent Shia Muslim and 5 per cent Christian.

Our day to day work includes regular foot patrols, mobile patrols using armoured personnel carriers, manning observation points and the control of traffic through the use of checkpoints.

Our role here is also humanitarian. Some of our officers have teaching qualifications and hold English classes in local schools. Needy local families are helped with financial assistance from the Department of Foreign Affairs and we support the orphanage at Tibnin. Also our doctors hold regular clinics in isolated villages and we provide patrols at harvest time to protect farmers working in the fields in frontline areas.

I'm greatly honoured to have several other Claremen serving here with me in Lebanon and my hope is that the Irish Battalion will do a thorough and professional job. Our aim is to continue to make a meaningful contribution to the safety and security of the Lebanese people in our area of operations.'

Radio Days
Eamonn O'Loghlin

Photographer Patrick McHugh

Eamonn O'Loghlin was born in Ennistymon in 1951. After graduating from University College Cork he went to Canada where he worked in marketing and communications for the Hallmark greetings card company before setting up his own consultancy business several years ago.

'I was educated at Ennistymon CBS. I have good memories of my time there. In 1964 I was sent to St. Flannan's College in Ennis on a five-year sentence. It was a tough station in those days with high walls all around it in case we might try to escape! We did get a great education there though, which I believe has stood to us all afterwards.

After Flannan's it was time for "Lockie" to go to University. After a somewhat uneven academic career, I graduated with a degree in Commerce in 1975. While in Cork I met Madeline Treacy, my future wife. She had grown up in Toronto, so when we got our degrees we moved over there, got married and figured we'd be back in a couple of years. Twenty-five years later and we're still here with two kids, Treasa, seventeen, and Rory, six.

My first job in Canada was with Hallmark Cards. By 1980 I was on the management team and by the time I went out on my own in 1994 I was in charge of communications for the company. Now, with my own firm I concentrate on marketing and communications for Irish and Irish/Canadian companies.

For the last three years I have hosted my own Irish radio show and I really enjoy Toronto's Irish scene. I visit Ireland once a year and really miss Co. Clare a lot. Over the last five years we've been so proud here of the Clare hurlers. I've watched every game live on the satellite and had the good fortune to attend the All-Ireland Final on 14 September 1997 when we beat Tipperary. I still have my ticket and some Croke Park grass to prove it!'

Desert Home
Marianne O'Connell

Photographer Veronica Nicholson

Marianne O'Connell grew up on the Limerick Road in Ennis.
She studied ceramic design and subsequently set up her own
pottery-making business before leaving for Dubai in 1987. She is
currently Head of Art at the Emirates International School.

'When I graduated from the Limerick School of Art and Design I set up
my own studio in the garage at home, producing handmade pottery.
I got married in 1986 and the following year my husband Olly was
offered a job in Dubai. He's a pilot and jobs were pretty scarce at the
time so we decided to go. The day we left I was carrying my daughter
Gráinne in my arms. She was just three weeks old. That's over twelve
years ago now.

I found life here difficult at the start. Coming from an "arty" background, it seemed Dubai was devoid of any kind of culture as I knew it.
I'm afraid coffee mornings with the other ex-pat wives just didn't do it
for me! So I set about finding myself a job.

I started teaching in the local Catholic school, St. Mary's, and then
moved to my present school, Emirates International, where I'm now
Head of Art. In the meantime I learned to ride horses, something I'd
wanted to do all my life. I even bought a horse in Ireland and brought
him out to Dubai.

I've also completed an MA in Education and hope to pursue further
studies. I love coming home and I get back to Ireland as often as I can.
I miss my family, especially my mum. But we have three kids now, so I
don't get much time to think about home. Also, being married to Olly
Conway means there are always the parts of at least twelve motorbikes
scattered around my house and there's usually a micro-light aircraft in
the back garden. Never a dull moment!'

After School
Colm Comyns

Photographer Christy McNamara

Br. Matthias Comyns was born in 1938 at Tarmon near Kilkee. After his profession as a Presentation Brother he spent some years working in Ireland before leaving for the West Indies. He is now retired, after a life spent teaching.

'I remember I was in my second year of secondary school in Kilkee when I heard a talk from a visiting Presentation Brother. I was very impressed and decided I wanted to join the order. Shortly afterwards I went away to the Brothers' school in Cork where I sat my Inter. and Leaving Cert. examinations and then did my novitiate training as a Presentation Brother. At that time I took the religious name of Matthias and have been known by that name ever since.

I spent some years teaching and then went on to University College Cork in 1961. I enjoyed my time there as the atmosphere was much more relaxed than in a secondary school. In 1964, I volunteered for the West Indies mission. At that time the Presentation Brothers had schools in Barbados, Trinidad, Grenada and St. Lucia.

Since then I've spent all my time here in Grenada, apart from a four-year stint in Trinidad. Although it's only about fifteen miles long by ten miles wide, Grenada is a very beautiful volcanic island with many mountains, rivers, and stunning waterfalls. Temperatures here are about thirty degrees throughout the year and the people are very friendly and hospitable.

I've spent all my time here teaching in secondary schools but I'm retired now. I still help out a little in the school and I'm involved in some extra-curricular activities such as scouting and hiking. I think about home now and again and about my parents, Michael and Nora Comyns. My brothers and sister are all still in Ireland and I keep in regular touch with them. They keep me updated on all the sports at home, especially when Clare are involved.'

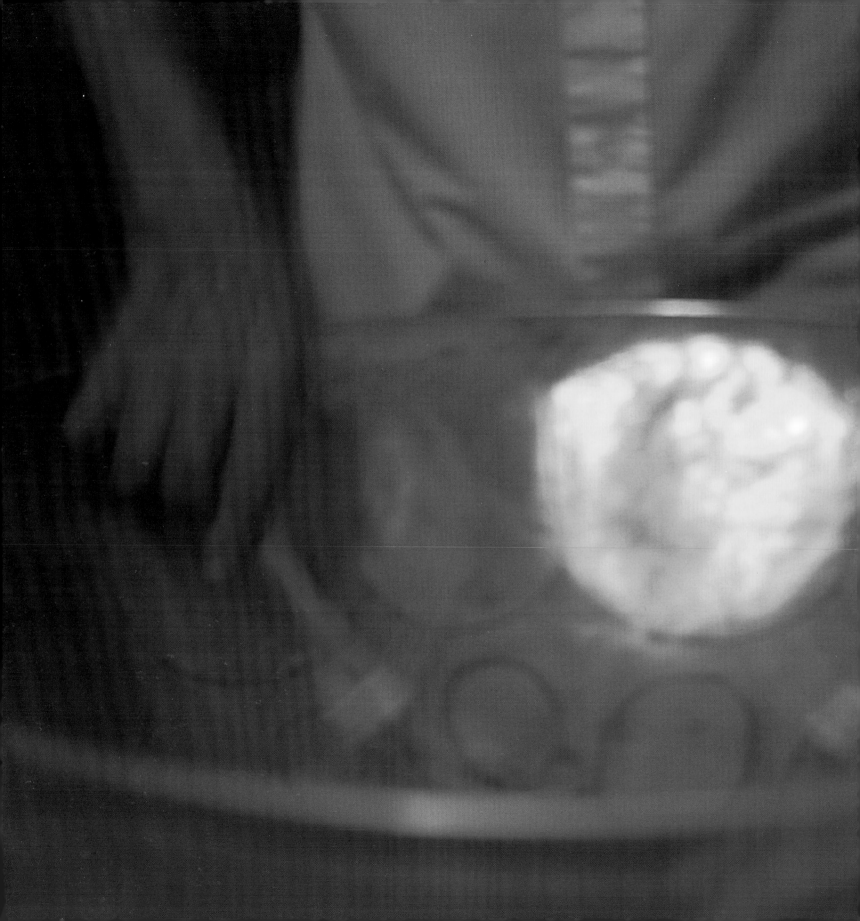

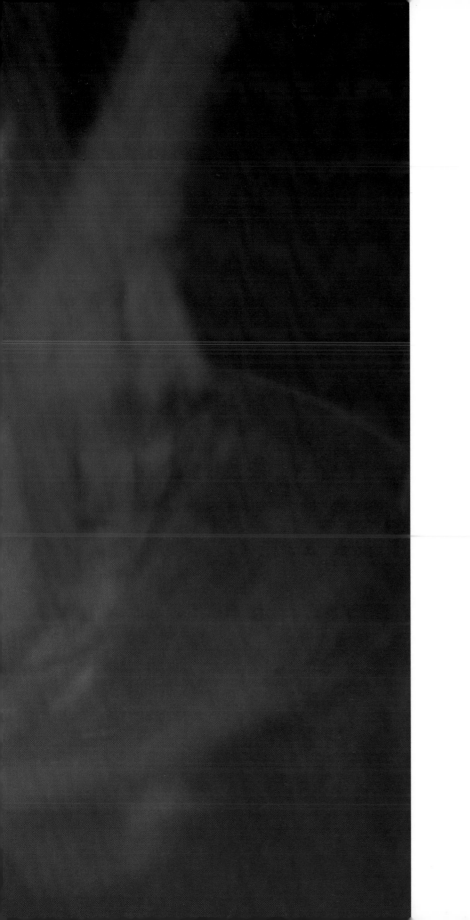

Paris Match
Eddie Casey

Photographer Eamon Ward

Eddie Casey comes from Ruan. After leaving school he studied electronics before going to Paris in 1990.

'I come from a family of ten so, as you can imagine there was never a dull moment. My late father Tommy was a hard-working farmer and most of his spare time was spent on hurling. We were born and bred with it. My mother was, and still is, a great cook. These days it's her brown bread and apple tarts that I miss the most.

After National School in Ruan I entered the long corridors of St. Flannan's. In French class the pictures from *L'Équipe* and *Paris Match* that covered the walls always fascinated me. It never occurred to me that one day I'd live and work in Paris. If it had, I might have paid more attention! Being on the Harty Cup Hurling Team has left me with some great memories. Training after school then thumbing home on the dark winter evenings, the build-up to the games, the battles with our arch-rivals North Mon and our ultimate victory.

After the Leaving, I spent a colourful few years studying in Galway before going to Paris. My brother Paul was already in France and my plan was to come for the summer, get a job for a few months and learn the language. Work wasn't hard to find and as time went by I discovered more about the French and their culture. After the summer I decided to stay on.

During the first few years I didn't have much contact with other Irish people here. Also, I really missed hurling. So a few of us got together and the Paris Gaels GAA club was formed. It's a sports and social club. We train on Sundays and go on occasional trips to play other teams around Europe.

I get back to Clare when I can. My most memorable trip was for the All-Ireland Hurling Final in 1997. I hope I'll be making a similar trip home again in the not too distant future!'

On the Banks of the Vistula
Padraic Coll

Photographer Veronica Nicholson

Born in 1970, Padraic Coll comes from Kevin Barry Avenue in Ennis. He studied accounting and finance at Dublin City University and qualified as a chartered accountant in 1994. In 1995 he moved to Poland to work in banking. He has since married and now lives in Warsaw with his Polish wife Ewa.

'I left Ennis in 1987 to study in Dublin. I got my degree in 1990 and decided to go on and do accounting. When I qualified I was looking for new challenges. I didn't want to end up in an accountant's office in Dublin for the rest of my life.

So when I received an offer to assist in setting up an Austrian-owned investment bank in Poland I thought I'd give it a go, even though I knew nothing about the country and couldn't speak a word of Polish. I left Ireland on a mild autumn day in October 1995 and I arrived here at the start of the Polish winter . . . it was already nine degrees below freezing. What a start!

As usual though, there was an Irish pub in Warsaw which was a great place to thaw out and meet other Irish people working here. There is a fairly big Irish population in Warsaw which means we all get together to watch the live GAA championship action during the summer. The rivalries can be intense.

Warsaw has a five-month winter but this is balanced out by a low cost of living, a relatively safe city, liberal pub closing hours and a real summer. Warsaw is a beautiful city built on the banks of the Vistula River; its historic centre was totally reconstructed after the war. When I came here first I thought I'd stay for two or three years but now the plan has changed. I met a Polish girl and married her in 1998. Needless to say my Polish is getting better every day.

I've discovered another thing too. Polish people, especially in the rural areas, are a lot like the Irish. This has made life easier for me here. Sometimes, sitting in a Polish farmhouse, if it wasn't for the language, I could imagine I was back in Clare.'

Lifting the Veil
Rebecca Conlan

Photographer Veronica Nicholson

Sr. Rebecca Conlan comes from Miltown Malbay. After leaving school she worked in the civil service before joining the Columban Sisters in 1967. She has served with the order in Korea and the Philippines and is now based in Hyderabad, Pakistan.

'Miltown was a great place for a child to grow up. At that time in the 1950s there was a carefree atmosphere around the town and I remember sitting listening to Willie Clancy play the pipes. After primary school I went as a boarder to Claremorris in Co. Mayo and then got a job working in the Department of Education in Dublin. It was a great opportunity and good experience but the Far East was calling me. So in 1967 I left my job and joined the Columban Sisters in Maghermore, Wicklow.

I trained as an occupational therapist in London and then I was sent as a missionary to Korea. My path led me to study pastoral work in the Philippines and then I found myself back in Ireland where I became involved in training young people for the missionary life. In 1989 I was asked by my order to go to Pakistan and the following year I arrived here with four others to start a new mission foundation. Pakistan is an Islamic state and life here for Christians isn't always easy. My work involves dialogue with Muslims, promoting justice and peace and training lay leaders. I also do a lot of work with families and help girls and young women prepare for their future.

It certainly is a long, long way from Clare to here but my treasured memories of growing up in West Clare with my parents Andrew and Josephine Conlan and my brother Paddy together with my friends and cousins and neighbours all keep me going. This was the cradle that nourished my dream to become a missionary which has taken me beyond boundaries of creed and culture to find a new home here in Pakistan. All these memories lighten my steps as I walk the dusty roads of Pakistan with the music of Miltown in my heart.'

[234]

A Time to Remember
Susan Clark

Photographer John Kelly

Susan Clark (nee O'Connell) was born in Burrane, near Killimer in 1913. She emigrated to England when she was twenty-four and then married a Yorkshire farmer. Later they moved to Suffolk where she now lives with her son John who runs the family farm.

'The 1930s were a bad time in Clare and the Economic War hit everyone hard. One day I saw an advert in *The Clare Champion* looking for a sewing-maid in England. It was for a family called Wright whose daughter was getting married and they needed a helper. So I decided to go. That was around 1937 or 1938. My mother wasn't happy about it but what could she do? We couldn't all stop at home.

The Wrights met me off the boat, and they treated me like one of their own. It was while I was working there that I met my husband John Clark. We were married on 25 February 1942 and Mrs Wright took me to the church.

We moved onto his farm and my first child Eileen was born later that year. My son John was born in 1944. My husband had always wanted to move south, he said it was too cold and wet up in Yorkshire, so in 1957 we came down to Norfolk and later we bought 145 acres here in Suffolk. John died in 1987. We were forty-five years married.

I never thought when I left West Clare that I'd end up as a farmer's wife in England but even so, I've worked hard all my life. After the children were born I didn't get home to Clare much and people used to say "We only see you when someone dies" and that was true, I always made it back for funerals. I miss my old friends and the good times we had when I was growing up. There are some Irish people in the area here and we sometimes meet up after Mass. But it's not really the same. You see, there's nobody here from my own county, Clare.'

A Clare Association
Bridie Shaw

Photographer Eamon Ward

Bridie Shaw (nee Moylan) was born in Inagh. She emigrated to London in the 1960s and soon became involved with organisations assisting Irish people in England. She is currently President of the Clare Association in London.

'I was over on a visit to my sister Mary in London when I saw an ad looking for a restaurant manager. Well, to my surprise I got the job and decided to stay a while. And that's how I ended up here in London. Then I met Paddy Shaw from Carlow and our first date was to go and see Ireland playing England at Twickenham. We were married in St. Thomas's Roman Catholic Church and now have a grown up son Fergal who works as a quantity surveyor. He's married to Tracy, whose father is from Cranny in Co. Clare. We have a beautiful grand-daughter Niamh who loves Irish music and watching Irish dancing videos.

I've been a member of the Clare Association here in London since arriving and went to my first dinner dance in 1965. I remember I had to spend a week's wages on the dress. The Clare Association was founded to help young Clare people coming over and to promote our culture and heritage. I have served on the committee as Assistant Secretary, Secretary, Chairman and now I'm President of the Association.

In the 1970s a group of us set up the London Irish Festival where Irish people in the city could meet and enjoy themselves and celebrate their culture. In the 1980s the festival attracted crowds of up to 100,000 and in the twenty-four years it's been running has raised nearly £2 million for charity. I'm currently the Chairperson of the organising committee. I have worked all my life over here in London and have never been out of a job. At the moment I am a sales representative for a large company but I intend retiring back to Ireland, please God, in the near future.'

Home to Kenya
Christy Burke

Photographer Eamon Ward

Fr. Christy Burke was born in Kilmaley in 1937. He was ordained a Holy Ghost Father in 1965 and has spent most of his missionary life living and working in Kenya.

'I'll never forget my first impression of Africa. I had landed in the steaming hot port town of Mombasa and found myself standing in front of the Cathedral. It was a massive stone structure dreamed up by some European architect and designed to keep out the rain, wind and snow. It has remained with me ever since as a symbol of how missionaries have sought to impose their own world view and experiences on other cultures and peoples.

My first few years in Kenya were spent teaching. Then in 1974 I went to Rome to do a doctorate in moral theology returning to Kenya in 1977. In 1984 I was appointed Chaplain at the University of Nairobi where I also taught philosophy. I enjoyed my time there and was sad to leave when I went to the United States on sabbatical in 1990.

The following year I returned to Ireland as a curate in the parish of Kimmage in Dublin and I thought my days in Africa were over. Then, when my mother died in 1992 one of my parishioners said, "That's it so, you'll be off again!" I didn't realise it at the time but he was right. A few months later I got a present of a ticket to Kenya. It was like going home.

Since returning to Nairobi, I've worked at the Catholic University, the Mukuru slum and been chaplain in the Mater Hospital. I also work with relief programmes for the communities who live in the slums around Nairobi, especially the women, some of whom have now started their own businesses making and selling craftworks.

In my present parish of Karen some of my parishioners live in extreme poverty while others are very wealthy. My challenge now is to bridge that divide, first with understanding, then later with energy and resources. That should keep me busy for the foreseeable future.'

Under the Cypriot Sun
Angela Ioannou

Photographer Veronica Nicholson

Angela Ioannou (née Flynn) was born in Miltown Malbay in 1954. After completing a course at the College of Commerce in Rathmines she went to work in London. While there she met and married Spiros Ioannou, a Greek Cypriot. They now live in Nicosia with their three daughters.

'I went to primary school in Miltown Malbay and then to the Convent of Mercy in Spanish Point. By the time I was finished there I was ready to see a bit of the world so I was delighted when I got a college place in Dublin. Boy, it was great to be young in the 1970s in Dublin!

After college I got a job in London and that's where I met Spiros Ioannou, the love of my life and my soulmate. We have been married now for twenty-one years and have been blessed with three wonderful daughters. We have lived in England, Africa and Egypt and now for the past fifteen years we've been here in Nicosia.

I'm very happy here in Cyprus but I would make a fortune if only I could figure out a way for County Clare to send us the rain and Cyprus to send the sunshine to Clare. I'm working on it but don't expect any miracles just yet!

Two of our daughters are still at school and the eldest is at university in England. We speak English at home so they are fluent in both English and Greek.

Summertime is always "Clare time" for us and that's when we head back. It's like the children's second home now because, since they were born, they have spent every summer there and know the place like the back of their hands.

We have a very active Cyprus Irish Society here so that none of us forget our roots. But for me anyway, despite all the countries I've visited or lived in around the world, I'll always be a Clare woman.'

Sweet Harvest
Maud Johnston

Photographer John Kelly

Maud Johnston (nee Murphy) was born in Kilmihil in 1914. She emigrated to Australia in 1928. After the death of her first husband she took over the running of his sugar cane farm, turning it into a successful business. She had seven children from her two marriages and now has twenty grandchildren and seven great-grandchildren. She retired in 1997.

'My first job in Australia was as an apprentice dressmaker but then the Depression struck and I was laid off. My uncle had a hotel in Queensland and he offered me a job. The work at the Kincora Hotel was long and tough, listening day and night to the Italian and Irish cane cutters, many with no work or futures, drinking away their troubles. I counted the days 'til I could save enough money to leave the place. Then I met Tom Dinan, a bachelor from Killaloe in Co. Clare and on St Patrick's Day in 1932 we were married. We had two sons, Patrick and Michael, but the day Michael was born his father died. So I was a widow at twenty-three, not knowing which way to turn. Tom had left me a cane farm, a house, a car, an overdraft and two children to rear.

However, I carried on. I paid the bills, raised the boys and learned to drive the car and tractor. The first year was the toughest and I was so glad when the time came to cut the cane. That was a sweet harvest! Soon I felt I had a grip on the business and then I met another Clareman, Tom Johnston. We were married on 8 May 1938. Life went on from one sugar season to the next and we had five children together. We also purchased five more cane farms plus the two at home which made seven in all.

The children are all grown now and I'm happy to say are enjoying a degree of success in their chosen ventures. Tom died in 1990 and I continued farming until a few years ago when I decided it was time to retire. I now live in a retirement village in Cairns near my daughters and grandchildren. The home farm is run by my son Bernard (Ducky) but I visit there as often as I can . . . just to keep an eye on things!'

Notes to the photographs

Page

List of Pictures by Photographers

JOHN KELLY: P. 24-27, 28-31, 52-55, 60-63, 88-91, 130-133, 146-149,160-161, 198-199, 238-241, 250-253

PATRICK MCHUGH: P. 32-35, 44-45, 50-51, 56-59, 78-81, 86-87, 96-99, 154-157,190-191, 204-207, 216-219

CHRISTY MCNAMARA: P. 40-43, 64-67, 74-77, 100-103, 118-121, 134-139,140-143, 158-159, 176-179, 180-183, 186-189, 222-225

MIKE MULCAIRE: P. 92-95, 108-109, 122-125, 144-145, 162-165, 166-169, 208-211

VERONICA NICHOLSON: P. 70-73, 104-105, 106-107, 128-129, 184-185, 212-213, 214-215, 220-221, 230-233, 234-237, 248-249

EAMON WARD: P. 36-39, 46-49, 68-69, 82-85, 110-113, 114-117, 126-127, 150-153, 170-171, 172-175, 192-193, 194-197, 200-203, 226-229, 242-243, 244-247